EMPATH Essential Survival Guide!

A Complete Guide to The Empath Blueprint, Overcoming Narcissistic Abuse, Reclaiming Self-Sovereignty, and Color & Chakra Therapy and Healing

GRACE GABRIELLA PUSKAS

✧

Please visit my Youtube Channel the *Dream & Spirit Weaver* for FREE educational videos, wisdom sharings, and spiritual/holistic/esoteric teachings.
(https://www.youtube.com/@TheDreamSpiritWeaver)

✧

ABOUT THE AUTHOR

Grace Gabriella Puskas is a spiritual author of two groundbreaking collections of poetry and a creative visionary. She is a qualified Reiki Master Teacher, Dream therapist, Crystal & Shamanic Healer, Chi Kung practitioner, Reflexologist, Aromatherapist, and Herbalist. In 2014 she won the Local Legend Spiritual Writing Competition, resulting in the publication of her debut book of poetry, 'A Message from Source.' Throughout her twenties she spent her time volunteering on various projects, spiritual, conscious, eco/sustainable, community, and animal welfare and conservation; she has lived on organic farms, shamanic land communities, and in ashrams, and has created beautiful Medicinal herb gardens, in addition to leading workshops in the Healing Arts & Spirituality. Grace Gabriella works at festivals and conscious community gatherings where she offers therapies, healing, and workshops aimed at spiritual development and accessing creative, soul, and intuitive/psychic gifts. She is a Teacher of the Healing Arts, Reiki, and Creative & Spiritual Development, and a poet, wordsmith, world-class ghost-writer, philosopher, inspired visionary, soul guide, psychic, empathic counselor, and astrologer. She is also a Pisces with a grand water trine and grand earth trine in her birth chart (two rare astrological alignments).

Grace believes we can transcend comfort zones by leaving behind a fear timeline, and moving towards a timeline of LOVE. Unity consciousness, authentic and conscious spirituality, holistic health, and healing planetary consciousness as well as Mother Earth, beautiful Gaia, are her main life goals and service. She is a Medicine Woman and free-flow Musician who embodies elements of a modern-day, grounded, mystic.

CONTACT:

gracegabriella33@gmail.com

https://gracegabriella33.wixsite.com/grace
https://www.youtube.com/@TheDreamSpiritWeaver

CONTENTS

Book Description

From low self-esteem and no boundaries whatsoever, to narcissistic abuse, energy vampires, and takers who seem to feed off of your light... Your journey as an empath is certainly not easy. You are a rare species, dear empath. Your destiny either through fate or free will (or a combination of both) involves transcending toxic cycles, clearing negative individual and collective/ancestral karma, and freeing yourself from the binding chains of society. In this book, you will find a complete exploration of the *Empath Nature*, how to heal and take back your power, and everything grounded and higher vibrational.

Empathy is not a weakness, despite what the world may tell you. From faulty belief systems in youth imposed on you to the patriarchal society that runs mainly on "left brain" and masculine qualities; logic, intellect, a focus on sport or physical attributes, competition, etc.- The *Empath Nature* is certainly overlooked. Not only is it overlooked, but it's ridiculed, misperceived, and underappreciated. Empathy is not valued when we're only looking towards physical beauty, superficial values, or how loud one can shout! Society encourages extroversion and intellectualism, while empaths run on instincts, intuition, and emotional depth, sensitivity, and intelligence. Fortunately, there is enough wisdom in this book to guide you on your path back to greatness. You are a diamond soul... It's time the world sees it.

Chapter 1: The Empath Nature

The Empath Nature: *An Introduction*

Being an empath is a beautiful thing. Empathy is defined by gentleness, purity, sensitivity, compassion, and selflessness; nurturing, emotional intelligence, and caring too. Empaths are arguably a new species of humans, homo lumens, as we operate at different frequencies. We empaths embody evolved emotional and spiritual vibrations, including emotional intelligence, maturity, and wisdom, as well as psychic gifts and spiritual powers. We're advanced. We're natural BS detectors. And we possess diamond souls.

In the crystal queen and kingdom, a diamond is one of the rarest gemstones. It's the hardest, formed over thousands to millions of years, under immense pressure, and is one of the most sought after. Diamonds are exquisite, and just like is taught in Buddhism, diamond consciousness is available to all humans. Empaths are most likely to reach this heightened state of consciousness and evolution. Unconditional love defines us. We embody universal compassion. We radiate innocence, joy, and wonder when on top form, and can do things only seen by unique animal species. From reading minds to communicating telepathically and speaking to animals to sensing things on a deep level, empaths are devoted to service. We live to be of service to others.

So, what is the empath nature?

The Empath Nature:

- Kindness, caring, selflessness, gentleness, and compassion.
- Purity, nurturing, emotional intelligence, sensitivity, and a strong sense of service.
- The ability to pick up on the thoughts, feelings, and emotions of others, in addition to mind reading.
- The gift of tuning into another's mood, inner state, inner vibration, health, wellbeing, blocks, fears, insecurities, hidden talents and gifts, and virtually everything inside; all beliefs, emotions, and thoughts can be felt, seen, and sensed.
- Natural lovers and givers, not fighters or takers! Also, a deep love and respect for and of nature, harmony, and inner beauty.
- Introspective, reflective, and femininely-inclined.
- Highly attuned senses, strong instincts, powerful intuition, and gifted in extrasensory modes of thinking, feeling, and perception.
- Warm-hearted with self-sacrificial and codependent tendencies.
- Amazing artists, musicians, speakers, listeners, storytellers, and counselors.
- Amazing healers, visionaries, dreamers, seers, clairvoyants, psychics, and natural caregivers.
- Magnetic, receptive, deep, telepathic, and multidimensionally aware.
- Inspirational with a need to replenish personal energy often. Empaths can lack boundaries, be people-pleasers, get drained easily, over-give, and over-trust.

Empathy Vs Being An Empath

How do you know if you're an empath or someone capable of empathy? Well, did you speak to animals when you were younger? Did you have lots of dreams that you knew, deep down, through your instincts and gut feelings, had deeper messages and guidance to offer? Were you someone who could communicate with plants, flowers, and the natural world, organically? Can you read minds, walk into a room and know, intuitively, what's going on without being told? Can you feel things, feel, see, and sense people's hidden fears, insecurities, pains, trauma, or joy, excitements, and victories?! These are some key signs you are an empath.

Everyone is capable of empathy, even narcissists, the most self-serving, self-entitled, and manipulative people this world will see. Well, actually, narcissists are capable of mimicking empathy! They don't actually embody it. Normal people, most people, can be sensitive, compassionate, and so forth. But to be an empath, your soul must have chosen before this incarnation that you would birth an elevated frequency, that you'd hold an evolved vibration to heal, help others, and be of service.

The Philosophy of Being An Empath: *Yin and Yang*

We can examine the yin and yang symbol, the duality symbol, to make better sense of the beautiful gift of empathy. Yin is darkness, feminine, receptive, magnetic, passive, and linked to the realm of emotions, feelings, and instincts. Yang is light, masculine, active, electric, direct, and linked to the realm of logic, intellect, and mind. Empathy is concerned with emotions, feelings, and instincts, moreover intuition, the subconscious mind, the imagination, and the spiritual, astral, and ethereal planes. The shadow self, which is essential for healing, self-development, and light integration, is linked to darkness or feminine energy. Empathy, compassion, nurturing, instincts, sacred knowledge, ancient wisdom, powerful subconscious insights, and all other empathic qualities are connected to the shadow lands, the darkness within and around. So, empathy is more "yin" than "yang."

If we look at the opposite of empathy, which we explore in chapter 2, we can see how everything contains a polarity. Without shadow work, deep and honest exploration of our darker attributes, we wouldn't be able to become enlightened. Spiritual illumination, soul-evolution, and subconscious and conscious harmony and integration wouldn't be possible. Philosophically speaking, empaths hold the light while narcissists bring only darkness, yet we *all* embody light and dark attributes. Yin or darkness flows into yang or lightness, and vice versa. Also, every human operates at a certain polarity; the amount of each is unique to each individual, based on their soul's unique energy signature or blueprint, etc. Your past, present, and future lives as pertaining to the Akashic Records, which holds your *complete* soul's memory and journey, give clues as to, 1. Whether you chose to be an empath in this life, and 2. What type of unique empath qualities, skills, and healing gifts you will have.

Below is the yin and yang or duality symbol:

YIN AND YANG/THE DUALITY SYMBOL

YIN	YANG
Darkness, emotions, and femininity.	Light, mind, and masculinity.
Magnetic, passive, and receptive.	Electric, active/direct, and dominant.
Subconscious forces.	Conscious forces.
Negative, repressed, and linked to the shadow self and realms.	Positive, expressive, and linked to logic, intellect, and cerebral powers.
Sacred knowledge, instincts, and intuition.	Self-authority, power, and sociability.
Nurturing, caring, compassionate, selfless, imaginative, and submissive; goes with the flow, surrendering...	Superficial, analytical, competitive, egotistical, "self"-focused, and innovative; self-leading, takes charge...
Astral, spiritual, divine, ethereal, and multidimensional power and consciousness.	Logical, intellectual, mental, physical, and creative power and consciousness.

All things exist in a polarity- yin and yang flows through all living things. Yet nothing is supposed to exist in an extreme forever. Energies, our personalities, and our likes, desires, and interests are supposed to flow, balance, and unify. Like the symbol for duality, yin and yang are designed to complement each other. If we look at narcissists, empaths' opposite, we can see that they are self-serving, superficial, and extremely egotistical. They appear to be of the light (yang), yet, deep down, miss out on a lot of beautiful qualities. Empaths embody yin energy, however they are not dark; quite the contrary, they are full of love, kindness, and grace to show and share. All empaths are emotionally intelligent, mature, sensitive, empathic, and wise too, and emotions are connected to feminine energy. So, this is all very useful to be aware of when exploring your own empath nature.

Empaths are masters of natural healing powers, psychic instincts, intuition, selflessness, and shadow work, and these are all born from darkness, from the divine feminine. Shadow work involves seeing the light and dark and then aiming to transmute and alchemize. People, like narcissists, who exist only in the light can't do this, they are too superficial, further only being concerned with their own needs. But those who have accepted and even made peace with their darkness (individual and collective) are able to be of service and shine their light... from the highest source. Empaths go in an up

(into the darkness, the individual and collective shadow) to come out and through; *enlightenment.*

Key Blueprints of the Empath Personality

The Artist, Creator, and Visionary

You are an artist, a natural creator with many artistic and imaginative gifts. In fact, all empaths possess at least one amazing gift, a talent or ability that, later in life, labels them a creative visionary! Empaths are so psychic, instinctive, and spiritually in tune that they can tune into the divine. You have a unique ability for tuning into the subtle, astral, and multidimensional realms for profound visions. Also, for universal archetypes. From a young age, you were more right brain than left brain. Your right brain relates to the free flow of thoughts and ideas, in addition to imagination, creativity, intuition, and multidimensional awareness. The left brain is more scientific and analytical, also concerned with linear thinking. Vision comes naturally to you.

Linked to such visionary and artistic powers is an active Third Eye. Your Third Eye chakra, chakra meaning "wheel" or "portal" in ancient Sanskrit is the seat of self-knowledge, power, intuition, psychic gifts, and spiritual powers. It links to the capacity for dreaming and receiving information from your subconscious mind. It's also connected to subtle perception, advanced cognition, and cerebral powers- intelligence, logic, wit, intellect, problem-solving and so forth. As a natural artist, you possess the unique ability of connecting to some universal archetype, idea, concept, frequency, or image. You can see through the veil of illusion. Your intuition coupled with your psychic gifts make you powerfully reflective, observant, and perceptive. Your imagination is off the chain... quite literally, there are no limits. Your ability to connect to something "above and beyond" makes you a natural at all sorts of creative, musical, and artist activities. This is only amplified through your emotional and spiritual powers. However you choose to express yourself, through song, dance, art, painting, drawing, poetry, writing, photography, film making, design or creative directing, you can achieve great things.

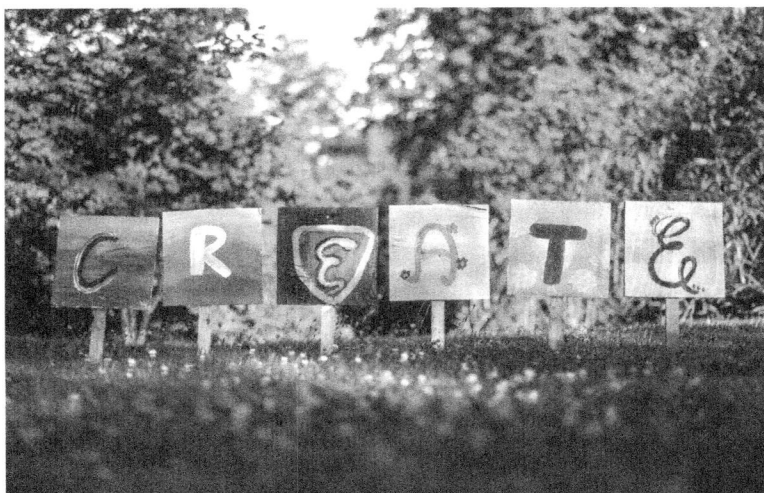

The visionary aspect to your empath nature can connect on an unseen and invisible level, enabling you to tap into divine insights and revelations. Mystical visions and previously unchanneled- unexpressed on the earth plane- concepts can come to you. The 3D realm is like an easy test you've mastered, empaths are able to connect to everything else, all the other dimensions, realms, and planes. You bring things forth from the subtle planes into the physical, making you an amazing channel. You perceive things differently to non-empaths because your Third Eye is active and awakened. Alanis Morissette is one of the most well-known musician empaths, and if you have not yet heard of her, you should check out her music. It's deep and inspiring. And that's what empaths are, deep, soulful, and inspiring. You're a natural change-maker and wayshower here to make the world a better place through your art. Unconditional love, universal compassion, and self-expression merge and entwine to come together in an energetic dance of the senses! You're a powerful co-creator who works with universal forces to inspire, educate, and uplift making. What a beautiful thing.

The Musician, Performer, and Storyteller

Closely connected to the above is being a natural performer, storyteller, and musician. Ok, there are some blocks and issues you need to work through first, like fear of shining in the spotlight, or blocks to speaking your truth, being bold and courageous, and having confidence. Empathy is a feminine gift, and feminine energy can be submissive, passive, and a bit shy and timid. This is only because you're so gentle and good-natured. You're not competitive, you don't want to outshine anyone or step over anyone. You're so talented, but you're also fair, loving, and just. Thus, it can be difficult for you to find your flow and groove, moreover "show off" in the way many others do. Once these blocks and fears are released however, you are a powerful creator, performer, and storyteller! Seriously, empaths have this unique skill of weaving golden threads and webs of ancient knowledge, mysterious words that heal and inspire, and magical cords connecting others. Empaths are magic-makers. They live with heart and soul, which allows them to do things mortals cannot. Oh yes, being so multidimensional and spiritual makes you in tune with eternal, infinite, and immortal energy sources and concepts. Your advanced emotional intelligence, sensitivity, and maturity sparks ancient echoes that heal and inspire. Your elevated spiritual knowledge and life force initiates self-talk and communication with the universe that many would call seer-like or prophetic. When applying this to music or storytelling, this makes you a magician. Magic-I-am, this is you, dear empath.

All thoughts, emotions, feelings, subtle sensations, and beliefs arise from the spiritual world. So do all mental constructs and virtually every aspect of consciousness that creates our individuality; thinking, feeling and interacting with others... communication. In other words, our emotions and thoughts arise from subconscious and subtle planes, which you are a natural master of. Everything exists as a unique vibratory frequency. Unlike others who may get a high off of video games, you get a high from music and storytelling. While others may walk into a room and instantly turn their attention to the xbox or similar, you would gravitate towards the plants or one or two people in deep conversation. *It's a natural resonance.* Your Higher Self is intact, which allows you to converse with others and the universe on a quantum and telepathic level. You thrive in the Arts or any career, professional path, hobby, vocation, or pastime which opens you up to new levels of imaginative thought, moreover playful expression. You're colorful, playful, and innocent- your inner child is awakened. You have a playful and courageous side after shy, timid, and reserved or overly modest and humble blocks are worked through. In terms of the inner child, empaths are so deeply imaginative, carefree, and joyous at heart, pure spirited too, that you emit beautiful vibrations that say, 'I treat everyone as my family.' Bob Marley's "One Love" is essentially the empath nature. You like to unify others, connect them through poetry, song, and music. Your voice is like poetry or music in itself, a healing tool for education and enlightenment. You can be non-invasive, passive, and impressionable, which makes you more loved than you know! You may think you're shy and unseen, your talents overlooked, but many people secretly admire you. You're magnetic beyond belief, and you don't seek the limelight, yet fame and prestige often seek you. You're genuine and sincere in your intentions and desires to be an amazing musician or performer. These intentions rippled into space... many empaths become famous.

Your ability to connect with unseen concepts, ideals, hidden emotions, impulses, and instincts, as well as the vast array of the human experience makes you truly captivating. You're inspiring and breathtaking. Furthermore, an empath fully stepping into their inspiring and motivating role is extremely confident and courageous- you literally have no fear! Emotions, personas, and expressions other people may be scared to show are your forte. You can merge with anyone and anything effortlessly. Even you will start to believe you are that character, a star, or the most shiny musician in the room. (But without ego...) You merge and entwine on a soul level, so you embody stardom. Music for you is a transcendental and mystical experience, even. As for merging in its entirety, if you choose to pursue a career in acting, you can play the role with excellency. Empaths are mind-readers, telepaths, and chameleons. You can express any emotion, frequency, concept, or story with your voice, music, or acting skills and so forth. You are a channel, a tool for the divine. Many empaths don't even need lessons or excessive training. Need I say more... Of course, if you do decide to choose a grounded path and go down the traditional route, dedicating your life to a talent, instrument, or artistic service and vocation will make you world-class and top in your field.

How do you do what you do? It all stems from love. Love is the strongest vibration. When people hear "empath," they think counselor, caregiver, healer, therapist, and so forth. These are all true, but you are also incredible and awe-inspiring artists. Your evolved emotional frequency and spiritual essence allow you to create with love, sensitivity, and enhanced self-awareness. You don't care for superficial things, fame, money, etc., although they do find you. Your intentions are pure, and purity births divinity. You're fuelled by the spirit of human connection.

The Dreamer, Seer, and Psychic

Something that is not often taught in schools nor accepted mainstream is the fact that you are an extremely gifted person. You are a dreamer, literally and metaphorically. As a literal dreamer, you can travel the multidimensional planes and dreamscape with ease. You are an avid or natural lucid dreamer, astral traveler, and astral projector, and are gifted with visionary and prophetic gifts. Empaths can explore consciousness with ease, slipping and merging between different worlds and planes. You are connected to subconscious wisdom and ancient knowledge, and deeply so. While some people may need to spend years training, attending numerous workshops, courses or retreats, or practicing lucid dreaming or astral projection for hours upon hours, many empaths can do this naturally. It can actually be quite infuriating to some. (Trust me, I had a non-empath friend who spent thousands of pounds on lucid dreaming and astral projection retreats and workshops, and despite his intentions, just could not do it!). Yet, to you it is as easy and effortless as breathing. Just like everything that was said with regards to you being an artist, creative, and visionary, your ability to access invisible realms and attune to your subconscious mind is extraordinary. Truly *extraordinary*. It is in dreams where subconscious messages, insights, guidance, wisdom, and universal or collective archetypes and imagery can be accessed. Your empathic nature allows you to do so in the most advanced ways.

Lucid dreaming is a form of "heightened and transcendental consciousness" whereby your conscious mind is awake and aware in your dream. It is essentially a portal into the dream and subconscious world and realms. Your mind is awake and present, instead of being unconscious, unaware, and asleep. Astral projection is the ability of being conscious and present in a meditative or transcendental state, or place "in between dreams and waking life." Your mind is free to wander and explore consciousness and spiritual, mystical, or subtle states of being, while you are simultaneously connected to your body. Astral projection allows you to access your subconscious mind, Higher Self wisdom, soul guidance, past, present, and future lives (wisdom, insight), and universal symbolism, archetypes, and insights. Your mind wanders the dream planes and worlds while feeling connected to your physical body. It is likely you have lucid dreamed and astral projected, dear empath. Astral travel is similar, only it's not only your mind that travels and explores, but all of you- your light body leaves the physical plane to explore the dreamscape.

Further, many empaths are natural seers. Extrasensory abilities, psychic gifts, potent intuition, spiritual powers, and clairvoyance are abilities you excel in. You may be a prophetic dreamer, whereby you see or predict future events in your dreams. You may be a prophet! Being attuned to an emotionally evolved and spiritual frequency in waking life allows you to see, feel, and sense things others miss. As a BS detector, you sense hidden manipulations, false intentions, and deceptions. As seer and psychic, you see invisible energy, picking up on clues and signals others miss. You are intuitive beyond belief; like a snake who senses subtle vibrations through the ether, you're a powerful channel for divine insights and ancient wisdom. Like a dolphin who communicates through supersonic waves, you're telepathic. Like an elephant who is deeply compassionate and empathic, feeling energy currents through the ground, Mother Earth, you are in tune with everything within and around; you're a psychic sponge. I hope you get the picture. Spiritual, shamanic, and advanced gifts are your domain entirely. Empaths have a powerful bond with spirit. This means you experience life and all it has to offer with extra dimensions. You're not just connected to the 3D world, you're in tune with many other forces and vibrations. Knowing things without being told, being able to tell when someone is ill or what specific ailment they have, and being able to suss out beliefs and opinions without being told are all common for you. You can instinctively sense what someone is about to say, when they're about to say it, when someone is about to ring or message, or when they're about to enter a room. Also, which direction the conversation is about to flow in. You have precognitive powers.

We live in an energetic universe where subtle vibrations influence and govern reality as we know it. This psychic sixth sense or seer-like ability arises from your deep emotional connection to others, yourself, and the world; you're in tune with the subconscious realm coupled with the realms of emotion, feelings, and instincts. This is where all thought, beliefs, and perspectives arise. So universal archetypes come naturally to you. Clairvoyance (clear seeing), clairaudience (clear hearing), clairsentience (clear feeling), claircognizance (clear knowing), telepathy, and psychic instincts are all possible, moreover highly likely as a "norm" in waking life reality. Referring back to astral projection and lucid dreaming, we all have an astral body, an aura, and a soul body. The astral body is active in empaths. The physical body is linked to the emotional and mental planes, which then connects to the astral body/plane. In between the denser bodies (physical/emotional/mental) and astral body there is the etheric body. This is an "energetic replica" of the physical body that transmits messages regarding health, well-being, and smooth or blocked and distorted energy flow. Above the astral is the spiritual body, which connects to the causal plane, and, finally, the soul body. Being aware of your subtle bodies is what deepens your connection to spirit, self-knowledge, and healing powers. The astral layer of existence is responsible for all links and connections to psychic, intuitive, and spiritual phenomena. Also, it is closely linked to your aura or auric field, which receives and transmits messages (for well-being, protection, gifts, etc.).

In sleep during dreams, your astral body is heightened and activated. So it's useful to be aware of its presence and work on strengthening it, techniques of which are given in chapter 5. The aura or astral body is where you can connect to dream worlds and your subconscious during sleep. So much wisdom, self-knowledge, creative genius, intuition, and dormant or unexplored gifts are available here. Think back to the information presented on the difference between empathy and being an empath. Empathy is linked to darkness and the shadow self, or the shadow realms; shamans and energy workers enter the darkest place of the human soul, through an activated astral body. They enter these darker places or the Unknown to heal imbalances and diseases. Without fearlessness, moreover comfort to enter the dark, they wouldn't be able to heal from the highest light or source. In lucid dream, astral travel, and astral projection, the cord or spiral connecting you to the ether, astral and multidimensional planes, and unknown is often dark. You must enter darkness, which signifies the complete absence of fear. Empaths possess unconditional love, hence why you can do this more effortlessly than non-empaths. While non-empaths may choose fear, consciously or unconsciously- the shadow and astral planes may be too much for them to handle, you, dear empath, choose love. Love protects you in an energetic cocoon, so you can travel dimensions. To get to the root where subconscious wisdom, higher guidance, divine knowledge, inspirational energy, and powerful insights are available, you must enter the Unknown; the Void, the Great Mystery... These are all rooted in darkness.

The Healer, Counselor, and Therapist

You are a natural healer, counselor, and therapist. You have something known as "healing hands" and "healing presence," coupled with impeccable listening skills. Most empaths go on to become a healer, therapist, or life coach or counselor of some sort. Healing is in your nature. You attune to such sensitive and genuine frequencies- thoughts, emotions, hidden beliefs, subconscious fears, trauma, pain, past memories, spiritual frequencies, everything going on below the surface; that you naturally take on the "stuff" of others. When unhealed and unevolved with weak boundaries, this can be dangerous. But when healed, balanced, and integrated with strong boundaries intact, this can be a beautiful pathway to a real profession or service. You possess extraordinary listening and counseling skills. You are able to connect to others on a deep level. You're able to look past all the superficial identities and labels and look deep inside, seeing someone's soul. You're empathic, compassionate, and caring without fault. You're selfless as well, which means you put aside your own needs and egotistical desires to help others. You're perfectly capable of acting in service to another's highest good, whether that be an animal, fellow human, or natural environment, place, or space. Empaths are masters of listening, counseling, and offering wise counsel.

As an empath, you find people gravitating to you, like sitting on a park bench and finding strangers coming towards your aura. You tend to be people's "emotional dumping grounds" when unhealed and unboundaried. Positively, people and animals trust you, they get pulled into your aura and energy field in a way that allows you to be your best self, sharing your talents, wisdom, and unique insights. People feel they can unload their problems on you because your aura is warm and inviting. It's non-judgemental, approachable, and welcoming- it speaks of family, sisterhood, brotherhood, unity, and tolerance. All empaths emit a specific vibration that sparks deep healing and remembrance, i.e. memory of being an interconnected and loving family. You treat everyone as your mirror, a reflection, and someone worthy of your time and love. So, people gravitate to you, sensing your tolerance, patience, and compassion. When applied to a professional setting, you can find great strength in the gifts you offer others. Your soul and heart are powerful. Your ability to give love and light, share wisdom, and offer wise counsel and pearls of secret knowledge and guidance are angelic. You possess a saint-like aura. Animals and children feel safe around you, while adults know they can look to you for sound, honest, and caring advice. There's no hidden motives with you. You radiate pure light, and this reflects in any healing or counseling service you offer, professionally or informally.

In terms of healing presence, you heal people through your presence and energy alone. Your aura transmits signals to others' auras, which sparks healing and personal awakening. Secrets come out around you, either consciously through the verbal cues you emit or subconsciously through how you make people feel. People feel safe, seen, and understood- your energy speaks for itself. Your aura says, *I am compassionate, I am an amazing listener, and I genuinely care about your feelings*. And, *Please feel free to share your issues and concerns with me; I am unconditional love personified*. Your advanced and deep levels of empathy allow you to read minds, feel feelings, tune into emotions, see things psychically or spiritually, and sense things without being told. Your intuition is so evolved its verging on telepathy. Any therapy, healing, or similar field is ideal for you as a career. As for listening skills, people see you as relaxed, easy-going, and supremely caring. There's no chance of threat, harm, or violence with or around you. You're heart-centered, meaning you live from the heart, as opposed to the ego or lower self/mind. Empaths also possess the ability of *holding space*.

The Animal Whisperer, Charity Worker, and Volunteer

Taking into consideration all the gifts and abilities shared so far, empaths make excellent animal whisperers. Also, charity workers and volunteers of any kind. Empaths possess something known as *inner*standing. You don't just understand things, you innerstand; you get to the root, to the core. Feeling others' feelings and putting yourself in another's mind, with compassion and sensitivity, enables you to thrive in any field or environment that requires depth and soul. As an animal whisperer, you can communicate with animals, asking them what their feelings and needs are. Your aura merges with their aura. You communicate without the need for words. You speak to them on a subtle and spiritual level. You ask them what's occurring and what their needs are, you listen to them. Animals are sentient, self-aware, and deeply empathic. They feel, experience real emotions, and live closer to nature than humans. Animals are beautiful creatures, so being an animal whisperer is ideal for you. Not only can it help to build confidence, but it can increase your empathic gifts further. Animal whispering is not as mystical or "woo" as you may originally think. Picture a dolphin, dolphins communicate telepathically through a special, supersonic radar. They use certain sound waves and possess the ability to speak to others of their kind through frequencies that are very real and accessible, yet we humans don't or can't attune to them. Now let's look at bats, some bat species use echolocation to "see" in the dark; they use soundwaves formed through echoes, which bounce off walls and other physical objects, to help them navigate, see, and sense.

Empaths have superpowers too. Oh yes, in addition to everything explored so far, animal whispering or animal communication is a very rare, but very real type of empath capability. Now onto volunteering and charitable services: empaths have BIG hearts. There's no-one quite as generous, kind, or sincerely devoted than empaths. Giving is in your nature, as is helping others. Choosing a path or career aligned to helping other humans such as the elderly, the disabled or disadvantaged, or some group or organization that needs help is a route many empaths choose to take. You tend to feel more comfortable around animals or in nature where you can just be yourself, or in any position that makes you act as a channel or conduit for healing... raising humanity's vibration, in some way. This is a huge aspect to being an empath, you seek to *raise humanity's vibration, contributing to the global and planetary shift in consciousness.* Charity, humanitarian, welfare, conservation, and environmental fields are suited to your highly sensitive disposition. You are genuinely concerned with the welfare and well-being of the earth, and all of her inhabitants. As stated with being a musician, artist, and creative, you have a gift for tuning into some higher reality. Higher perspectives, including powerful morals and ethics, come naturally to you. Anything aligned to these vocations will help you to shine in the most brilliant ways, bringing out your best characteristics.

The Carer, Social or Support Worker, and Elderly Companion

Connected to being a natural healer, counselor, and therapist is your innate tendencies, moreover drive, to take on a caring role. Many of the caregivers, social and support workers, and elderly or animal companions you see today are either empaths or have strong empathic tendencies. As one of the most selfless, genuine, and generous souls to walk this planet, there's no role more suitable. This is an ideal career, volunteering, or life path choice. *You're a giver. You seek to create meaningful bonds. You love to help people. You live to be of service too. Your whole identity is wrapped up in the connection you have with others...* Your advanced emotional, spiritual, and psychological frequency allows you to thrive in such vocations or professions, so definitely consider this, dear one.

The BS Detector, Spiritual Healer, and Intuitive

Being an empath naturally brings an element of spiritual awareness into your daily life and existence. Natural beauty appeals to you greatly. You love nature, music, serenity, sensuality, silence, peace, and harmony. You are intuitive and wise beyond your years. You have a gift for seeing the good in others, you're full of grace. Many empaths can pick up on the energy and even history of a space, for example a building, sacred site, natural place, or object. Everything contains a memory and empaths are in tune with the spiritual-energetic space of a site, object, or place. You pick up on subtle and ethereal frequencies. You're connected to the subtle and energetic life force of all things, the interconnectedness. Your sixth sense and psychic muscle is advanced. Many empaths become tarot readers, psychics or clairvoyants, spiritual teachers, healers, shamanic practitioners, sound healers, reiki masters, multi-therapists, tantric practitioners, astrologers, dream therapists, or metaphysical teachers. You actually know things without being taught or told. You're a natural BS detector too, which signifies unveiling hidden truths, uncovering secret knowledge, and discovering secrets, lies, and manipulations.

Some empaths can pick up a book and receive certain downloads of information. Some of you can go to sleep with a book or journal by your pillow and receive wisdom, knowledge, and information contained, through dreams and subconscious guidance. As an empath, you can see through the veil of illusion, get to the root of fear, BS, pain, deception, and internal blocks- in Self and others, and unravel life's meanings and mysteries. Empaths despise liars, you're so sincere and heart-centered that truth is more important to you than lies, even if it hurts! Empaths are used to pain, crying is not something you're ashamed of. Any spiritual, healing, or metaphysical, multidimensional, or psychic path can benefit you greatly.

Holding Space: A Natural Empath Gift!

Holding space is staying centered, balanced, and self-aligned within to be a channel for others. When you have self-control over your personal vibration, you can assist others in raising theirs. Through staying centered and aligned with the other person's (or animal's) healing in mind, you can raise their vibration through your own energy. This is done through a combination of *intention* to raise their light, shift stagnant or blocked energy, or contribute to their healing, and self-mastery. You consciously direct the conversation and energy flow. Eye contact, emotional self-control, spiritual and holistic (mind, body, emotions, and spirit) self-mastery, and subconscious clues, which is achieved through the intentions you emit, are how you do this. To hold space is to put another's needs above your own, being totally selfless while acting without ego. But, to also not sacrifice your boundaries. Self-respect, self-love, and personal boundaries, to maintain your own light and life force, are essential. It's about selflessness (positive/healthy), not self-sacrifice (negative/unhealthy).

When you hold space you dedicate your time, attention, and energy solely to the person you are seeking to help. There are no selfish motivations or hidden intentions. You're not being disingenuous, nor are you serving your ego. To hold space is to emit, channel, and reflect divine light, healing, and life force to another. You can help them remove blocks, overcome fears or trauma, get to the root of repressed emotions, and explore hidden and subconscious desires, memories, triggers, gifts, talents, and strengths. Through eye contact, self-control, and intention merged with directed energy flow, you become a powerful healing presence. You can hold space for an individual, an animal, or a group. Many empaths master this gift and hold space on a planetary level, such as upping their vibration to such an ascended (self-mastered) state that they serve the collective. It's a wonderful thing to be able to do, hence the name *homo lumens*; those who are of the light. The empath nature is one of the purest expressions of love any human could hope to achieve in a lifetime. It's angelic, saintlike, and divine.

EMPATH BLUEPRINTS: Core Qualities, Skill Sets, and Character Traits

The Emotionally Mastered Empath

This is the core empath frequency, the empath blueprint from which all other empathic qualities arise. Everything described in 'Key Blueprints of the Empath Personality' are birthed from your unique level of emotional self-mastery. You're emotionally sensitive, deep, empathic, aware, wise, and mature. You're spiritually evolved, perceptive, and wise. You operate on a unique frequency. Emotional harmony, balance, and self-control can overcome chaos and disparity, so this is something you should work on. Keeping your emotional body cleansed, clear, and pure is essential on your path. Your emotions are here to serve you, and as your whole identity is entwined with the emotional connection you share with others, in addition to the emotional healing you bring to others, it's paramount that you work on your toxic traits. Even empaths have toxic traits, shadow traits to transcend and let go. A lack of boundaries, codependency, and people-pleasing, the inability to say no to others, are linked to this. Emotional mastery is your key to healing on all levels, working through painful cycles and limiting chapters, and finding your true place in the world.

The Environmental or Plant Empath

Environmental empaths are intrinsically connected to the plants, trees, flowers, and natural entities of the world. Like an emotional empath who can tune into others' emotions, you have a unique ability of connecting with plants on a deep level. You have a natural intuition about what plants and flowers need, being attuned to their energy fields. You just know, instinctively, and tend to speak to your plants or nature itself. You might not need to read a book on specialist wisdom, like how to grow or care for a plant or flower; the knowledge will flow to you from the Great Spirit, from Source. You additionally find seeds and plants grow in your presence. You will walk into someone else's house and instantly gravitate towards the plant, being told that it needs water or to be repositioned. Plants, like people and animals, respond to energy and subtle impressions, and many plant empaths make great shamans and healers due to the ability to feel the spirit of the plant. You receive guidance from trees and flowers, and are further able to communicate with them on a telepathic level! As an environmental empath, you have a fine-tuned sense of the natural wonders of the earth. You can sense and get a read on physical locations, natural objects, and places of energetic significance, like sacred sites. They have a special resonance to you and you may be able to feel things beyond the physical senses from stepping into a place, for example, a holy site, a temple on sacred grounds, or places like Stonehenge. Environmental empaths are also known as *geometric* empaths due to the geographical element of their gifts. Natural objects such as gemstones, crystals, and rocks can be connected to, to receive information. Additionally you sense and feel other people's emotions, memories, and experiences when stepping into a place. You become a compass, in tune with the natural world and all of its wonders...

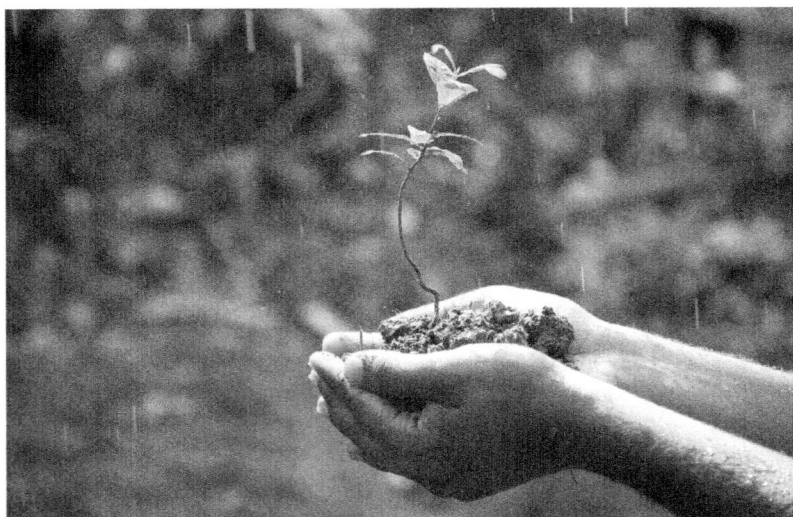

The Physician or Telepath

Psychic or medical empaths take on the physical ailments of others. Like an emotional empath who absorbs the emotions of others, psychic or medical empaths pick up on the physical state and energy of other people's (or animals') bodies. This can present itself in many ways such as through physically taking on the symptoms, aches, and pains of another. Or through picking up on it astrally and seeing or sensing what's wrong, inside, like a blockage or ailment/disease. For example, feeling like you have a pain in your leg when someone else has a pain in their leg, or briefly getting headache symptoms when near someone with a headache. Or by taking on symptoms of stomach ache when someone has stomach ache. The same can be true for toothache, painful periods, and pregnancy... The list is endless. Blockages, ailments, distortions, wounds, and imbalances become clear to you. You are a psychic sponge, a natural physician, and a telepath. This is achieved through extrasensory perception combined with strong and powerful intuition.

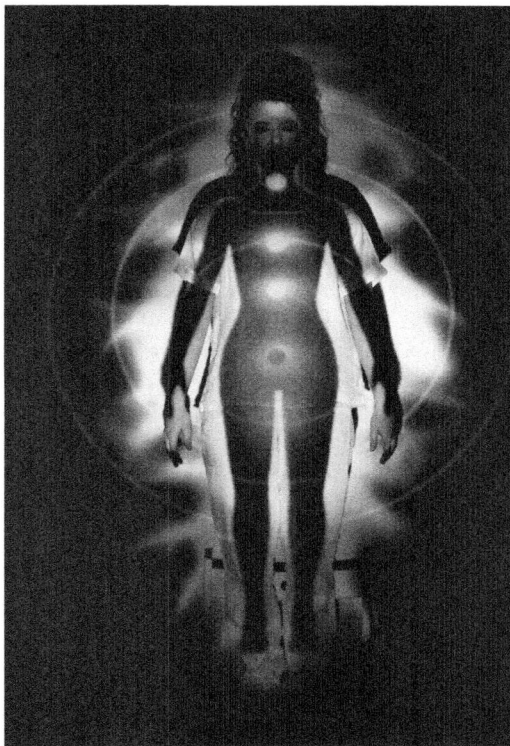

The Intellectual Empath

The intellectual empath is an empath who functions on a strong psychological frequency. Intellectual empaths gather and store information similar to a computer... or creative genius! Empaths are sponges with a deep and genuine connection with others; you absorb or are receptive to the power of collective energies. So, in terms of intellectual empathy, you merge emotional intelligence and maturity with psychological depth and intuition. Some examples include tuning into memories and past experiences to help others, through merging with their auric field. You can do this with an individual's mind or group's mind. Other people's energies, thoughts, and intentions affect you deeply. You're able to see as well as help others move through emotional barriers, through advanced mental powers of observation and perception. Also, reflection, problem-solving, and fine-tuned vision. Amazing authors, writers, poets, speakers, spoken word artists, lecturers, publishers, teachers, and researchers possess the gift of intellectual empathy. World-class experts in these fields go on to lead and inspire, through living with heart combined with intellect, logic, and wit. This involves courage, self-leadership, and strength, masculine qualities that are very different to the foundation "empath frequency," which are feminine. Logic, intellect, and cerebral gifts are masculine by nature, whereas emotions, feelings, and instincts are feminine.

Thus, intellectual empathy is quite unique, and something not all empaths possess. Emotions and spirit are yin, watery and passive in nature. Air is yang, direct, assertive, and expressive. You might read a book and store all the information on a subconscious, and then find it comes out at the perfect time. You can mimic conversation, communication style, and even dialect or accent. Like a parrot, you can mirror and reflect hidden qualities, but this time on an intellectual level. Your mind is like a cosmic holographic computer. When you need it, you "pull" information gathered from previous times, learning opportunities, and experiences out of the ether or your subconscious. This can be used for inspirational words and works of art, counseling others, or being of service of any kind. When you next interact with someone who needs your help, some subtle energy triggers your mind into knowing the perfect thing to say, at the perfect time. You know about some seriously complex topics! You might visit a place and receive psychic downloads of information that you later use. Intellectual empaths excel in the realm of communication, speaking, writing, storytelling, and talking; you use a combination of all feminine gifts explored so far, and combine them with boldness, courage, innovation, cerebral power, and higher cognitive functioning, as well as problem-solving, analysis, logic, wit, and fine-tuned perception.

You can mirror behaviour or knowledge, taking it out of another through merging with their energetic auric field. This is not a manipulative tactic nor birthed from dishonesty, a real empath would never steal another's work or ideas. But it's your own words and wisdom, as it's come from deep within, from another time when your subconscious stored it. This is how powerful your Higher Self is. As an intellectual empath, you can easily change vocabulary, speech, and style to different people, further from all sorts of backgrounds, cultures, countries, ethnicities, and communities. When communicating with others, you may just change roles or personas and start speaking of unusual, specialist, or expanded subject areas. It's instinctive, psychic, and intuitive. You can essentially adapt to any character, language, or culture with ease and effortlessness. Your self-knowledge is advanced, your mind and emotions are harmonized, and, like a parrot, you mimic with exquisite excellency. As it's instinctive and intuitive with a lot of help from your subconscious mind, you may literally ask yourself, 'how did I know this?' It's an ingenious gift to have. Furthermore, the wisdom you bring into the world may have been read, heard, or absorbed from 2, 8, or 12 years ago.

The Activist Empath or Soul Warrior

Activist empaths or soul warriors, if you resonate with this empath archetype, you are a powerful creator! You love to help others, live for service, and act out humanitarian, idealistic, or charitable desires. You possess a unique type of masculine self-leadership, which could be down to your personal Numerology or Astrology blueprint (your life path or the planets in your natal heart). You strive for justice, truth, and peace. You live for harmony, social cohesion, and making the world a better place. You are courageous, bold, and devoted, disciplined, and full of purpose and passion too. You still take time to recharge and connect to your inner source of power, but you are also strong in your beliefs and convictions; you harness your empathy to do good in the world. Many activist empaths go on to become campaigners, politicians, leaders, or speakers, in addition to channeling their abilities into some creative or artistic field with a big picture focus. You are a visionary and changemaker, and you believe in standing up for the underdog, living fearlessly, and taking risks. You do everything with grace, soul, and integrity- you're supremely modest, humble, and noble. There's no such thing as violence or sacrificing your integrity and internal moral compass. If you choose a more assertive path, it's to serve others. Activist empaths are true soul warriors with hearts of gold and an appetite for social unity, justice, and cohesion. Moreover, your spirit is strong, you're unbreakable with equal amounts of faith and humility.

Empath Myths and Misconceptions

1. Empaths are over- sensitive, weak, and hyper-emotional.

One of the greatest misconceptions to being an empath is that you are weak. Confusing kindness for weakness is one of the biggest mistakes done by narcissists, takers, and other toxic characters. Your sensitivity is not a weakness, it's a superpower. Empaths tend to get abused due to this misconception, with people believing we "deserve" such gaslighting and horrible treatment. Why? Because we're too kind, too trusting, and unconditionally loving? What a twisted mindset. Sensitivity and kindness being seen as a weakness are what lead us to being abused, which, in turn, perpetuates karmic cycles. Being melodramatic is linked here- people often think we're melodramatic because we feel things so deeply. But feeling, empathy, and emotions are not dramatic, on the contrary, they're what make us peaceful and serene. Empaths are deeply tranquil and peace loving individuals, yet we're often perceived as dramatic in our responses and beliefs. I am sorry to sound so crude, but I am a changemaker and an idealistic visionary: this myth is on par, from my perspective, with the rather disturbing statement: "justifying eating animals 'becasue they taste good' is like a rapist justifying rape because 'it feels good.'" Many empaths are vegetarian or even vegan. Yet when they try to bring some sanity, moreover humanity and compassion, to friends and family, they are met with stupid statements like this ("well, animals taste good, so f--- compassion!")

Empaths are some of the strongest people on this earth, we just have some issues including shyness, sensitivity, and weak boundaries to work through. A real truth is, many people are extroverted and rely heavily on external distractions, like constant social events, instant gratification, and entertainment that dulls the brain. Many people become human doings, while empaths are human beings. We enjoy being present, finding deeper connection, and intimacy that nurtures, nourishes, and connects.

2. Empaths are shy, anti- social, and introverted.

We are far from shy or anti-social, yet many people perceive us as these things. Why is this? Well, we live in an extroverted society, which signifies masculine traits are emphasized and prioritized. Empaths are shy and antisocial when in our shadow selves, we are lone wolves who enjoy our own company and solitude. But once we are healed, balanced, and evolved, we're not shy at all. We appear so because we emit an angelic frequency. We are relaxed, open aura-ed, and masters of holding space for others. We often appear full, lifeless, or passionless, yet this is just because we're self-mastered. I am not being biased! It's the truth. While others may be pulled into chaos or drama, entwined in false stories, endless distractions, and constant negativity or distorted frequencies, empaths are quite chilled "doing nothing." We do nothing, simply holding space and being cool, calm, and serene because we know that everything arises from the empty space. Everything comes from nothing, so our shyness, silence, or reservation, is, in fact, a place where miracles, magic, and wonder are born. Further, communication isn't always verbal, we communicate subtly, instinctively, and telepathically, therefore we don't need to always speak. Silence is where all sound, music induced, arises. It's in silence and stillness where true wisdom, mastery, and beauty are found and increased. Narcissistic or loud and overly gregarious people don't seem to understand this. You can feel high, happy, or energized from observing and reflecting, connecting to others on a subtle level. You don't like gossip, pointless chat, or excessive communication just for the sake of speaking, so some people see you as anti-social. In fact, you despise these things.

As for introversion, this is quite a common myth. Reflective, introspective, and quiet are *not* the same introverted. Yes, many empaths are introverted, but many of us are also introverted-extroverted; balanced. To be introverted is to be totally reclusive, yet empaths love to share, inspire, be inspired, express, and show off their colorful, creative, and empathic personality.

3. Empaths are self- centered and self- absorbed.

In complete contradiction to the last myth and misconception is the fact that some choose to see you as self-absorbed and even selfish. Wow. Empaths?! The world's most giving, selfless, and unconditionally generous people alive? This is clearly a misconception. Selflessness is the opposite of selfishness. We're misunderstood, that's all. I want to share one personal story with you (the only one in this book...). In youth, I used to do a lot of space holding and multidimensional dream work. A huge percentage of my teenage years was simple meditating, being, and dreaming- things I knew intuitively were essential for my and planetary healing and well-being. I needed a lot of time to be still, explore, refelt, contemplate, and find myself. I needed to be a channel, essentially, putting the collective's needs above my own. I fasted a lot, didn't do "normal" things a teenaer in society would or should have been doing. My mother didn't understand me, and, as it's a twisted world, used to call me selfish. I guess she thought I was just sleeping (for hours, days, weeks, and months on end... really?!). I was in my multidimensional holographic chamber, immersed in the spiritual realms, and clearly trying to heal and ascend. Yet she didn't understand the unique vibration I carried, and so called me selfish. It did trigger me, I must admit. I was being totally selfless, in fact, if we're getting really honest, my personal, love, and social life suffered. Immensely. So this 'selfish' statement couldn't have been further from the truth.

Perhaps you have a similar or the exact same experience! We empaths live in a different world (plus worlds) altogether. We vibrate at unique frequencies, and our multidimensional light bodies are active. We find solace in the astral, dream, shamanic, shadow, and subconscious planes and worlds. To society, this isn't normal- many of the things we can do aren't even seen as possible or attainable, however real they are to us. There's a lot of distorted and twisted energy in play, in addition to faulty belief systems. Many people don't see you. They don't see or understand you at all; some of your most beautiful qualities including unconditional love and compassion, deep care, and empathy are misperceived. They may not even be received due to the *shield* many wear. People put blocks up, they choose not to see. I had a dream about my own cousin back in 2012 that was quite dark and disturbing, in terms of his coldness and authentic, lacking all love, feelings towards me. I didn't understand it at the time, but did after we became estranged 10 years later...

A prime representation of this myth is the following. You are sitting in a room silent, introspective, and empathically connected. You have entered into a social gathering or situation with intentions of deep and authentic connection, being the friend in need or consciously opening yourself up to be ready to give advice, love, and care. What a blessing your energy is! This is your vibration, it is you in your realest without any mask or facade. Yet, to loud, narcissistic, and emotionally closed off or extroverted characters you are appearing self-centered. Quite simply, you don't exist on their frequency, thus they can't see you. They have put up a shield to your truth and empathy because they have most likely closed off this part of themselves, or at the very least not consciously worked to integrate it. They may be overly masculine or aggressive or simply used to attention-seeking and spotlight-seeking displays of social behavior. *You operate on different frequencies*. Another example is that you shine in the most selfless and unconditionally giving way possible to mankind, yet people see you as selfish or manipulative. They can't understand that you truly are a giving, kind, and authentically love- fuelled character, so your actions and motivations *must be* selfish; you *must* have a hidden agenda. This "must" is, of course, their own ego illusions and projections. Many people have distorted beliefs coupled with patterns of thinking.

4. Empaths are lazy and lack drive, ambition, and passion.

Ok, firstly, empaths can lack passion and drive, because these are masculine qualities. Yang qualities need a lot of work and integration. Empathy as explored is a gift often derived from the silence and the space. The "silence and the space" is the emptiness of being, the source of creation, pure consciousness, the Unknown, and so on. Empaths are not lazy, nor are they passionless; they are introspective, humble, and quiet. They only communicate when it's necessary- endless gossip, banter, and mindless conversation just for the sake of being social are not interests or passions to empaths. We don't chase fame, money, or status either, so it's easy to create the assumption that we are ambitionless. The true empath personality is defined by a need for deep connection, intimacy, emotional bonding, harmony, and compassionate relating. Also, by being selfless and of service, so quite the contrary to misperceived beliefs, empaths have immense drive. There are lots of intentions that consume the empath mind, moreover they put a lot of pressure on themselves, to be of service, heal and help others, and so forth. On the other hand, empaths may become temporarily lost in the reality of literally becoming a caregiver, counselor or therapist to virtually everyone, so it is easy to assume we are "lazy." It's not that we're lazy, it's just that we're attuned to a different reality. Being of service to others, being everyone's free therapist or counselor, and lacking boundaries can create a lot of illusion and confusion, specifically regarding what we do with our time. Some people don't take our intentions or passions seriously!

5. Empaths are always depressed, melancholic, and moody as hell.

One of the empath shadow trait sets is being depressed, melancholic, and moody, this much is true. But, this is not our core frequency, this is just a shadow trait we have to transcend. Extroverted, narcissistic, and superficial people, aka always upbeat and falsely positive or overly zealous people tend to see silence and down time as something dark or negative. Here's a secret: empaths love silence, the shadow realm, and down time. They find comfort, solace, and wisdom in darkness, silence, and self-reflection. People who are always up, social, and fakely positive can't access deep avenues or subconscious wisdom or insight and knowledge from the shadow self. Subtle and psychic impressions are few and far between, because everything is so superficial, chaotic, and expressive. An empath can sit in a room full of people, when mature and healed (boundaries intact) and reflect, tune into people's auras, and receive powerful downloads, as well as navigate both the conscious and subconscious realms. This is why they are so wise. Quiet time combined with introspective tendencies are perceived as moody to many people. Being reflective or mellow is seen as depressed. Outside of the actual empath shadow traits, which are here to be transcended, empaths are very colorful, imaginative, and positive people. We're just not superficial, fake, narcissistic, extroverted, or shallow... Any tendencies we empaths do have towards isolation and withdrawal is to recharge and rejuvenate, so we can be with friends, family, and our community once again. Taking on the problems of others as a psychic sponge or, in worst case scenarios, an emotional dumping ground, can leave empaths moody and down. Yet, this is temporary, it's not a forever frequency.

6. Empaths are mentally ill, crazy, or have serious psychological problems.

Chronic Fatigue Syndrome, headaches, insomnia, nervous tension, and other physical and mental health issues and ailments *can* arise in empaths, and it is important to be aware of this. But sassinging such things to us is a myth, not truth. In some cases, empaths can suffer from the effects of being everyone's doormat or emotional dumping ground, or from taking on too much, being overly generous and trusting and so forth, and having diminished self-worth and boundaries. However, these are not the actual empath personality. Empaths are magnets to narcissists, get pulled into other people's sob stories and dramas, and tend to be projected upon. People's twisted and distorted plots and games pollute an empath's auric field, making them question themselves. Empaths will be gaslighted by narcissistic and false-motived people at least once in their life. Being an actual or free healer, counselor, and therapist to friends and family is also a key route to being depleted, being gaslighted or projected on, or being directly or subtly abused... All of which can lead to cold and callous, quite simple, mean and "evil" spirited, people labeling poor empaths crazy. Because empathy is primarily an emotional gift and quality, your perceived problems may stem from emotional manipulation of others or through the very same love and care or compassion you project. Any pattern of thinking, belief, or perception that is not true, in addition to being essentially self-created, faulty, and distorted, is a *distortion*. Distorted mindsets are what lead to empaths' unconditional love, compassion, and sensitivity being ridiculed, persecuted, or used for horrible intentions.

Remember, just because you hold certain intentions and motivations in life it doesn't mean everyone else does. Being an empath is a very unique and often intense experience; one profound myth is that we are psychologically damaged or mentally ill, when, in fact, we vibrate at a much higher frequency than most people in society. We are above society, in many ways and respects. Linked to this is unconsciously taking on other people's karma through being too kind, as well as people-pleasing. By giving compassion to truly heartless and cold abusers or users, you forgive them and release them or try to release them from their karma. This is also known as self-sacrifice. Yet, in the real world, outside of the empath's supreme kindness, generosity, and selflessness, this doesn't work. Everyone must pay their karmic debts, eventually. Although the empath will try to sacrifice themselves for another, as they are the epitome of unconditional love and compassion, after all, the universe always steps in. The empath is always divinely protected with infinite angelic and celestial support around them. The people they are trying to "save" must face the music, and when they do this releases the empath from their mental prison. Oh yes, this is one thing normals, narcissists, and non-empaths do get right; empaths do live in a mental, psychological, and/or spiritual prison, there is a certain level of manic depression, psychosis, or craziness about them. *Through a lack of boundaries*, empaths suffer coupled with taking on the world's problems, and this leaves them open to psychic attack, harmful intention, hate, persecution, destructive projection, and unkindness.

There's no world, reality, or paradigm where making fun of someone so pure and angelic is right or justified. Pushing one when they're already down, further, belittling, verbally attacking or slandering, abusing in any way, or causing further pain and suffering when they know empaths are soft-hearted and sensitive... These are considered "evil." Evil is not supported by the divine, God, the archangels, or the universe. Empaths may be weak, lacking assertiveness, prone to bullies, and more polarized to prey than predator, but is this an excuse to become a bully or persecutor? I think not. Some people in this world don't understand how their words and actions affect empaths, and therefore themselves. Society likes to put empaths in the crazy box, without realizing how much it affects them in the long-run. There are karmic repercussions to abusing, ganging up on, or persecuting a genuine and sincere empath. Again, empaths are this world's earth angels, saints, and soul warriors! Placing such a strong sentence (crazy, mentally ill, etc.) on us only comes back to haunt those passing the sentence.

Misunderstood Behaviors

Other Misunderstood Behaviors linked to Empath Myths include:

Holding Space: Detaching and becoming seemingly "aloof"

To hold space is to muster up all of your might, energy, and courage, and become strong and centered within. Then, to direct and channel it for others. Many empaths do this, and frequently, but to do so you must detach from the frequencies and stories many people know and are used to. For example, playing murderous xbox games, watching football, binge-watching t.v. series, laughing about serious and traumatic subjects, and engaging in endless and mindless chatter, gossip, and communication. Holding space selflessly with an angelic face is clearly alien to a lot of people in this day and age. So, when it's seen, heard about, or observed, people receive it with ridicule, shock, and ignorance. Ignorance is to ignore, ignoring the validity and truth of things. The beautiful miracle that is holding space, in such an elevated frequency, is seen as being aloof or completely strange. Well, empaths are the oddballs and black sheeps! Seriously, the miracle and magic of embodying such an ascended and evolved frequency is met with disbelief, faulty perception, and total ignorance. People think empaths are super-spacey, lost in dream and fantasy realms, and aloof verging on idiotic. Well, one of Albert

Einstein's most famous quotes is: "Everyone is a genius. But if you judge a fish on its ability to climb a tree, it will live its whole life believing that it's stupid."Empaths may be prone to spaciness and disassociation, mainly in youth and when still working through key toxic traits; remember that the two astrological signs associated with the empath nature, are Cancer and Pisces, and their shadow traits include hypersensitivities and hyper-emotionalism, as well as self-sacrifice.

But, not everyone understands space holding or the unique vibration you carry, and for those people who are actively against healing and self-development- they prefer their bad habits and toxic and karmic cycles; they can misconstrue your intentions and personal energy altogether. The key word here is projection. People *project* their own insecurities, faulty or distorted belief systems and ignorance onto you. The best analogy to use here is in relation to sound wave frequencies and natural phenomena. Dogs and many other animals can hear parts of the sound spectrum that we humans can't, but it doesn't mean that these specific frequencies and high or low pitched sounds don't exist. Thus, you appear aloof, detached, or disconnected from your physical environment, when the reality is you are more connected than most.

Appearing cold, unfriendly, and anti-social

Empaths need their alone time and solitude, we love our "little bubble," where we can heal, find wisdom, and be reflective. Also, be creative, find our artistic talents, and hone in on our empathy and spiritual gifts! But, we are not anti-social, we just need to be around the right people. Empaths are very social around the right people. Empaths are actually 'introverted-extroverts,' our true natures and personality are expressive, creative, and very courageous, at least when it comes to helping others and speaking up for social justice, unity, and cohesion. We're pretty fearless, despite our initial shy and overly humble personas. We may appear cold, uninterested, bored, rude, unfriendly, and lacking all passion and life force altogether. At least, this is how we're viewed from distorted eyes. Truth is, we're extremely self-controlled, so much so that we may be considered self-mastered. When mature and evolved, we can hold space for ourselves and others in a way that allows us to be a master of our emotions, thoughts, feelings, observations, memories, and connection to the world around us. We don't need to show off, we're not attention seeking. We don't seek the spotlight or seek to win and outshine others at all costs. We're supremely humble and gracious in social scenarios. There's a level of sophistication and respect, although we may just see ourselves as sensitive and spiritually in tune! We need our alone time, we love our solitude, and it's true that we need to recharge a lot, to regain our strength coupled with our energy reserves. Yet, we are not anti-social; we're just selective and self-mastered.

Empath Toxic Traits to Transcend (Release, Heal, and Let Go Of)

Unlike empath myths and conceptions, this section is rooted in truth. As an empath or highly intuitive person, you will have to come to terms with your own toxic traits. Just like a narcissist, you also have shadow traits, otherwise, you wouldn't be so drawn to them. *All empaths display them at some point in their lives*, especially when younger, in youth, and before exploring your personality in depth. These are key to navigating your own innate powers, as well as stepping into self-alignment, personal power, and wholeness and ultimate living, living your best life.

1. People-Pleasing, Appeasing Others, and Lacking Boundaries

The first category of empath shadow traits is an inability to say no coupled with a lack of boundaries. All empaths have a real people-pleasing nature, which means they appease others. You over-give, over-share, and are too generous and loving to the point of burn-out; you deplete yourself through the innate desire to give, heal, help, or share. You want to give all of you, every cell of your body. It's admirable, saintlike and angelic even, but it's not sustainable. You bend over backwards for strangers and loved ones, give away all of your money, time, and energy, and get used and often abused or taken advantage of in the process. Empaths are the people strangers will walk up to and unload all of their problems on, because, 1. They send you have a heart of gold coupled with amazing wisdom to share, and, 2. They sense you are a push-over. I am sorry to say it, but it's the truth; you're a pushover and doormat who people use to unload and project all of their issues onto. You're so emotionally and spiritually evolved, in addition to being a psychic sponge, that you become people's wall or mirror. Not everyone is as kind, genuine, or selfless as you, these are traits not shared by all of humanity. Being aware of these toxic traits are the first keys to healing and evolving.

2. Self-Sacrifice, Codependency, and Being Everyone's Doormat

Being everyone's doormat, codependency, and self-sacrifice and core to the empath shadow self. It's very easy to become codependent with such a high need to be of service, help, and heal, moreover constantly give your empathy and compassion away. In your desire to nurture, lovingly assist, and offer your sage wisdom, heart, and evolve emotional frequency to others, you become codependent, or people become codependent on you. Simultaneously, you tend to people-please- appeasing everyone at expense of yourself. This ties into self-sacrifice, one of an empath's worst traits. You sacrifice yourself, literally putting yourself in "emotional dumping ground" or "doormat who can be used and abused" status. It's not good. It ruins your self-esteem, drastically decreases your self-worth, and ties you into narcissistic characters in a severely detrimental and destructive way. Self-sacrifice leads to diminished joy, happiness, and play, and once these qualities decrease or diminish, it's more likely to get attracted to narcissists and other abusive characters. Simultaneously, depression, insomnia, and minor to major health imbalances occur as a result of self-sacrifice leading to diminished joy.

Remember that empathy is rooted in emotions, instincts, and feelings, which are energetically speaking 'yin qualities.' Feminine energy in a lower vibration gives rise to depression, mood swings, and holistically, a lack of joy, passion, playfulness, fun, and positivity. *This is why narcissists feed off of your light, because they **always** need to be upbeat, positive, and joyous whereas you don't mind being mellow, introspective, or in a "darker" vibration (from society's perspective). You're also not superficial, therefore your depth, authenticity, and honesty is what makes them steal your energy.*

When you sacrifice yourself, your opposite type of person, the narcissist, steals, cheats, and cons. On a level, you've given them permission to, because you've said, "my energy is open, free, and without boundaries." You exist in a polarity when your toxic traits are unhealed, so users, takers, and people without heart or empathy feel it's ok to treat you in such disgraceful ways. Sacrificing your 'Self,' your entire being, opens you up to terrible and inhumane behavior. Always wanting to give without receiving (love, healing, etc.) also opens you up to mistreatment. It's a hard truth to accept, but you do create this on some level; even empaths, the world's most loving, giving, and kind-hearted people, deserve some tough wake-up calls if they don't love or respect themselves enough. Luckily, this is not your end story! It's just the first or a few chapters until your lessons are learned.

3. Social Anxiety, Fear of Large Crowds, and Panic Attacks

Empaths often suffer from panic attacks, especially when young. This is because you feel everyone's pain, picking up on all the coldness, harshness, and injustice or brutality of the world. Even watching the news or seeing horrific scenes in movies can be extremely distressing. As an empath, you absorb the pain, suffering, and coldness of the world because your core nature or motivation is to heal. Your psychic and sensitive capabilities make you know, instinctively and intuitively, that you can help. So, this is what you're fuelled by, it's inescapable and undeniable. Large crowds can be very upsetting, and you prefer one-on-one conversations or connections, or small groups with a few close trusted friends and allies. Social anxiety is strong, as you pick up on all the psychic impressions and sensations around you. Panic attacks, hyperventilating, or pausing in the street to return to your center (every few seconds) is common for empaths. You may have developed agoraphobic tendencies when younger. Excessive worrying about your health, fear of getting ill, and irrational beliefs about eating, health, and well-being are core to the empath toxic self. Unlike others, the reasons for these extreme beliefs are unique. You believe you must starve yourself in the form of fasting to keep your spiritual vibration high, or be "perfect" to always be ready for service, healing, or helping. This is why *boundaries* are so important, they're your superpower, or should be...

4. Hyper-Emotionalism, Super-Sensitivity, and Excessive Crying, Worrying, and Pessimism

There's nothing like the empath sensitivity or emotional depth, wisdom, or vulnerability, or, when at your lowest, the empath hyper-sensitvity. You can be hyper-emotional, prone to mood swings and depression, and a real cry-baby, bless your sweet heart. You are prone to excessive crying, worrying, and pessimism, negative thinking that puts you in a deep and dark spiral. In this spiral, you succumb to self-denial, neglect of personal needs, a lack of self-awareness, impracticalities, and regret, guilt, and self-blame for all the people you didn't help. Oh yes, if you're truly an empath, you will have at least 10 (possibly a hundred) nights alone in your room thinking about the copious amount of humans, mammals, sea creatures, and even insects you failed to help along your journey. You are unconditional love and universal compassion personified.

If we're referring to astrology, the empath personality is similar to the Cancer and Pisces personalities. Cancer and Pisces are both the empaths of the Zodiac, so you can explore these two star signs for deeper understanding and wisdom. Cancer is prone to codependency, extreme super-sensitivities, and self-sacrifice, least to mention mood swings and depression, while Pisces is known for being supremely impractical, ungrounded, and self-sacrificing, in addition to hyper-emotional and lacking all boundaries. Pessimistic thinking ensues. You become negative, only attuning to all the things you *haven't* done, as opposed to all the wonderful acts you've done. This is a toxic trait you need to let go of.

5. Isolation, Addictions, and Low Mental Health

Like Cancer and Pisces, empaths are prone to addictions and extreme isolation, also known as *Lone Wolf Syndrome*. Empaths are lone wolves, at heart, incredibly introspective, introverted, and in need of a lot of solitude. You need to put yourself in your bubble, so you can evaluate, contemplate, introspect, align, and recharge. In fact, no-one needs as much alone time for healing and clearing as an empath. You absorb so much, which interferes with your personal energy field, that it's essential to take time out from the world. But, you also take this too far and become a Hermit, isolated and withdrawn. This then leads to illusory fears, irrational or destructive belief systems, and social anxiety coupled with going within yourself. Relationships suffer. Self-esteem diminishes, and self-worth is eradicated. In your need to withdraw, recharge, and isolate, you cut yourself off from society, the world, and possible future community groups that would serve your soul, moreover family. Addictions can take over, like food, self-pleasure, or drug addictions, or you may fall into a polarity like dual sign Pisces. This signifies denying intimacy and physical pleasure then getting lost in the world of self-pleasure or porn; rejecting normal healthy foods, in your need to fast or detox to keep your spiritual vibration high, and then "pigging out" to make up for lost energy; or any other extreme.

6. Everybody's 'Free Therapist and Healer'

Empaths absorb the pain, trauma, suffering, and feelings of others, so you become the other person, animal, or plant entity, in a way. It's much different to normal people who may have empathy, empaths *actually merge with another's energy field*. Thus, every single hidden energy current, cell, and vibration, no matter how subtle, can be seen, felt, and sensed. Empaths are natural clairvoyants, clairsentients, and clairaudients, as we explore later. Empaths can read minds, communicate telepathically, and go inside another through evolved hearing, feeling, and sight. This means that in the pursuit to help or heal, uncovering hidden pain or trauma, or talents and abilities if they wish to bring out someone's strengths, an empath will play free therapist, counselor, or healer. This has many negative repercussions. Firstly, not everyone wants this free advice, no matter how wise or accurate. This opens you up to projection, negativity, hate speech, persecution, alienation, or even psychic attack. You equally create some negative karmic repercussions for yourself, specifically linked to a lack of boundaries, overgiving, oversharing, and giving your professional opinion without consent or request. Why 'professional?' Because your strengths are linked to real careers and service pathways later in life.

Secondly, in your genuine desire to get to the root and source of imbalances or ailments, you become a free healer, counselor, or therapist. Those people who do want your help and wise counsel become dependent on you, relying on you to the point of codependency or burnout. This then makes you less free, independent, and self-sovereign, as well as wrapped up in the stories and pains and trauma of others. The direct result is further burnout, mental exhaustion, and, somewhere down the line, isolation... due to the social anxiety and immense pressure you've opened yourself up to. Eventually, you become so entwined and attached to the stories and pleas for help from others (your gifts are extraordinary) that you fall into depression, melancholy, or despair. You believe the world to be a dark place, your mental health has suffered, also neglecting joy, personal passions, and intimacy in the name of serving others and self-sacrifice. Don't be fooled, being everyone's free therapist, counselor, or healer is not a glamorous thing. On the contrary, it's quite dangerous.

Chapter 2: Everything You Need to Know About Narcissism

A Deep-Sea Dive Into Narcissism... Empathy's Opposite

To explore or ascertain whether you truly are an empath, it's useful to look at, 1. The ins and outs of narcissism or someone with Narcissistic Personality Disorder (NPD), and, 2. how narcissists treat empaths.

The Story of Narcissus

Narcissus was a Greek god of Roman mythology, son to the river God Cephissus and the nymph Liriope. Narcissus made countless women fall in love with him, devoted to him. He would accept their sincere and genuine offerings of love, smiles ,and affection, and then smirk and snigger at their suffering when he rejected them. He was wholly arrogant, unkind, and self-centered, moreover horrible, cold, and heartless in his dealings. He was so self-centered that he died falling in love with his own reflection. You heard correctly; he would spend day after day staring at himself in the

---

water, in love with himself (in an unhealthy and non-self-loving way) that this extreme level of pride and self-admiration killed him.

Narcissism and NPD Characteristics

1. Selfish, self-serving, and self-entitled

Notice all of these begin with "self." Narcissists are selfish, self-entitled, and self-serving without any empathy, humility, or remorse. It's all about them, being number 1, while empaths are givers, not takers. Narcissists seek to take, draining you of your energy, time, love, care, money, resources, devotion, and "insert every beautiful quality here." Empaths are givers, narcissists are takers. Someone with NPD only looks out for themselves, feigning kindness, morality, and nobility. They are massive pretenders! This is how you know you're an empath, your intentions are sincere and actions are genuine.

2. Egotistical, arrogant, and incapable of modesty

Narcissists take arrogance to a whole new level, being egotistical, prideful, and vain beyond measure. It's all about me, "me, me; me." They shout, slander, abuse, ridicule, and deflect accountability in extreme measures to get their way. They're incapable of modesty, humility, or empathy, basic human kindness and consideration. A narcissist will be standing in the center of a room or crowd commanding attention, while shouting about sh*t, actual made up cr*p. Yes, it's serious. Narcissists are so arrogant that they live in a make-believe world of stories that don't make sense and aren't real. They are egotistical to the point of extreme vanity, false pride, and self-delusion; they put themselves in an illusory bubble whereby they believe their own stories. Think back to the story of Narcissus.

3. Insensitive and lacking all empathy and compassion

Narcissists fein sensitivity, empathy, and compassion while not showing any real emotions. They are masters of mimicking human behavior, expressions, and emotions, like a parrot; they can imitate, mimic, and copy. This is wrapped up in their social facade, the mask they display in public. Behind the scenes, they will be emotionally and psychologically abusive, volatile, horrendously unkind and immoral, and use you, their partner, family member, or friend, as a verbal punch bag. You are their emotional dumping ground. They hide behind your empathy and understanding, moreover your tolerance, patience, and supreme compassion. Your unconditional love is a shield to their abuse, whether more direct or subtle. The story in private is completely different to the story in public.

4. Unkind, unjust, and immoral

Narcissism is defined as a total lack of empathy. There's no fairness, justice, or equality in relationships. While you give, narcissists take. While you are a lover at heart, narcissists are fighters and haters. They're full of hate, envy, venom, spite, jealousy, rage, and uncontrolled emotion. Morals and ethics are non-existent, it's all about what they can take and how they can use people. Your energy is used for personal gain, moreover selfish motivations.

5. Extreme gaslighting tendencies

Narcissists use extreme gaslighting tactics to control, manipulate, and gaslight their victims. Gaslighting is twisting and distorting reality at extreme measures. To be gaslighted is to believe you're crazy, that reality is, in fact, not real. Gaslighting involves twisting real-life events, facts, words, speech, and actions to make the victim, aka, you, believe you're crazy. Gaslighting involves a repetitive type of psychological and spiritual warfare coupled with psychic attack, bombarding you with false information and threats. Additionally, emotional manipulation and blackmail are strong. Gaslighting is a primary tactic for narcissists seeking total control, in addition to maintaining their false social mask and facade. Through fear, intimidation, and repetitive psychological abuse aimed to make you feel crazy, they are able to maintain their illusions. This keeps the cycle of narcissistic abuse in play.

6. Self- delusions and inner traumas masking as confidence or self-esteem

Narcissists convince them and everyone around them that white is black and black is white. From a philosophical perspective, yin may flow into yang and vice versa, but there are boundaries and barriers in play. Like Narcissus, narcissists have a strong wounded inner child. But unlike most humans, least to mention empaths, they refuse to heal or change. They don't want to evolve, they wish to remain in their self-created delusions forevermore. Why? Because this is how they create power and gain followers and fans. Inside, narcissists are weak and vulnerable wounded children who never got the love and care they needed. *Yet*, before going any further, take note. Your compassion runs deep, and I would never advise not giving empathy or compassion to others. However, narcissists are attuned to a whole other frequency altogether. They do not give the same energy, love, or kindness back; quite the contrary, the more you give the more they take. *Narcissism is a personality disorder*, and like with sociopathy, psychopathy, and other mental health disorders, it's self-destructive to continue pushing for gold.

7. Notions of grandiose, superiority, and righteousness

Narcissists cause immense pain to those they claim to love, as when it appears there is finally light at the end of the tunnel, they will return to their vicious games. They are self-righteous without fairness or morality, superior without common sense, intuitive power, or rational thought, and attuned to a grandiose vibration where they are the clown dressed in a business suit making everyone around them feeling inferior… but this clown is an evil clown with a chainsaw! If their amazing storytelling fits don't work narcissists will resort to verbal abuse, belittling, slander, and even physical threats. They are intimidating, bullyish, and brutish without a sense of fair-play. It's their world and everyone is their subject. This is a true story for people with NPD. They sincerely believe everyone to be beneath them, existing solely for their pleasure. They may choose a few close friends and supporters who will reinforce their stories and false intentions when their BS has been exposed in a public setting.

In other words, when people are discovering something isn't right, smelling a rat, as the saying goes, the one or two followers- sorry, "friends," who they have give some love, energy, and genuine warmth too will back them up, telling all the doubters (intuitive people who can sense their manipulations) how real they are. *Narcissists are master storytellers, con-artists, and manipulators.* They distort truth and seduce or entice people to play along. At the end of the day and when the long game is over, even the people who have been their saving grace will be disposed of. Narcissists are all about number 1.

8. "The Empath-Narcissist Dance" or Karmic Entanglement

Finally, one sure way to know you're dealing with a narcissist is how they entwine you in their evil plots and schemes. They are insincere, sketchy, and sociopathic verging on psychopathic, 'extreme narcissism' is in fact another word for people with strong sociopathic and psychopathic energy. Be under no illusion, narcissists dream up sincerely evil plots, schemes, and plans to anielate others. They will choose someone as their target and then go on a year or decade long war against them, sometimes this war lasts until death (and then gets taken to the next life based on such bad karma accumulated). Their victims are targets, emotional dumping grounds, and doormats, and their venom is so strong that they need everyone else to believe their false stories and deceptions. Lies, gossip, intentional truth distorting ("sh*t stirring" for those less mindful…), and putting you down when you're at your lowest or weakest is common. They entwine you in something known as the empath-narcissist dance. It goes like this:

1. You give all of your love, devotion, time, energy, care, wisdom, resources, soul, etc.; the narcissist takes.

2. You start to realize that the energy and love isn't reciprocated, you question, pry, and ask for greater harmony.

3. The narcissist either, 2. Dismisses you entirely, acting cold, unkind, and heartless, or, 2. Feess you with false promises and false intentions.

4. This cycle repeats, alternating between the two possible reactions explained in step 3. Over time, you begin to question your worth, sanity, and will to live. Many empaths become depressed or even suicidal, or start to feel imprisoned by their narcissistic partner. All hope is lost, there's an undeniable feeling of entrapment, moreover inability to escape.

5. Despite the zero love, empathy, and care, you become codependent on the narcissist. Their false promises or brief moments of love and affection or connection become your hope. You "cling" onto their manipulations and false charm, always believing there are brighter times around the corner.

6. This cycle repeats for months to years or decades. It's a lonely and dark place to be. Finally, picture the image of a princess enclosed in the top room of a tower. She becomes attached, magnetized, and mesmerized to the idea and *fantasy* that she will be saved, that her knight in shining armor or prince will come for her. *This is all she has, false intentions given to her by a sadistic predator, hope, and blind faith.* This is the empath-narcissist dance.

I am not demonizing narcissists, but you do need to be aware that it's not something taught mainstream today. Therefore it's not something known or understood for what it is. Dare I say it, narcissists are a different species of human, at least when considering that *empaths* are destined to evolve and transform into *homo lumens*, majestic and noble beings who exist on a frequency of light, sharing their powerful wisdom, extrasensory abilities, and elevated emotional and spiritual frequency for the benefit of mankind or planet earth's ascension. There are two main timelines, a timeline of love, unity, and universal compassion, and a timeline of fear, separation, and distorted consciousness. Empaths operate on a timeline of love white narcissists are attuned to fear. In our personal lives and on a larger scale, this has many serious implications because our intentions, thoughts, and emotions ripple out. We're powerful creators, shapers, and influencers of our destinies, yet we equally affect the realities of others. This is why it's so significant to be aware of narcissism and NPD traits, as well as heal yourself through the activities and techniques outlined later...

As for karmic entanglement, if you attach yourself to a narcissist coupled with their immoral plots, schemes, and evil plans for so long, you inevitably take on their karma. It may not be conscious, at first, yet the more you support, agree, and comply the more you become a spitting image of them. This isn't true for when you are a victim- all empaths are victims to narcissists! Empaths can be seen as prey while the narcissist is the predator- they prey on your innocence, trust, and naivety. However, in cases where you have decided to lower yourself to their level, you can take on some of their karma. This is especially so and more true for the narcissist's fans and followers, the people who join in on the abuse or ang culture bullying mentality. Perhaps only a rare few souls, other empaths, or highly intuitive people see through their games and BS.

Here are some final key things to look out for:

"Normal" Relationship	Relationship with a Narcissist
Affection, raw or vulnerable emotion, deep and sincere feelings, respect, mutual cooperation, authenticity, and honesty.	Manipulation, emotional deception, gaslighting, white or severe lies, arrogance, pride and egocentricity (on the narcissist's behalf).
An emotional desire to be close intimately, romantically, and sexually.	The emotional desires of exerting their will and making you feel small or down. Wanting you to be powerless, jealous, confused, intimidated, vulnerable, fearful, angry or frustrated.
Mutual feelings of trust and respect, harmony, and desires for a commitment, family, or marriage.	Little to no real respect (there may be an illusion of respect present when in social settings), plus no intentions for a real commitment. You are their property.
Thinking and feeling in terms of a partnership; values such as cooperation, communication, empathy, consideration, harmony and 'we' are present.	'Me,' 'mine' and 'I' often replace 'we' and 'us.' There is little to no consideration of actually being in a *partner*ship.
A sense of inspiration- both partners inspire one another to be the best versions of themselves, or at least support one another.	A genuine lack of care for their partner's (your) self-development, happiness, success or personal goals and dreams coming true. It is all about them.

"Narcissists and Normals:" Why You Are the Perfect Match for the Narcissist

Here are five major reasons why you are the perfect match for a narcissist.

1. Potent Magnetism

There is always some magnetic quality that draws you together, whether that be their *charm*, apparent shared interests, or simply your empathy. There is truth in the saying 'opposites attract' and a narcissist is, fundamentally, the polar opposite of empaths, due to their complete lack of empathy, sincere emotion, and inner moral compass. Your personal magnetism is irresistible, but, unfortunately, it becomes fuel to their narcissistic personality over time. You become their energy source, and this leaves you drained, depleted, and traumatized.

2. Feeding their Personality

You feed them. You feed their ego, you feed their narcissism, and you feed their motivations for wanting to inflict pain, suffering, or sadness on another. Of course, you aren't responsible for their behaviors or feelings- it is your natural self that feeds their narcissistic personality. Any positive or lovely quality you possess is fuel to their out of control, burning, and destructive fire. A lot of it is unconscious too, at least at first, until you become karmically bound or entangled to them, at which case, damage is already done.

3. The Need to Thrive off Others (to keep their illusions in play)

The need to thrive off others to keep their illusions in play is common. Illusion is a word strongly associated with narcissism and something you unconsciously play to. *Delusion* is also accurate. A delusion is an idiosyncratic belief, recurring thought, or impression that contradicts reality, further rooted in some sort of mental imbalance or faulty perception. A narcissist needs this not only to thrive, but to survive. Their whole reality is dependent on it, furthermore they need others to keep their delusions intact. They achieve this through the fear, intimidation, and harm they cause to others, moreover the codependent-narcissist dance their targets or victims become entangled in. Narcissists require fans and followers. No, not friends, but minions to reinforce their stories and mind games when their narcissistic supply is weak.

4. Deception and Manipulation

Narcissists are so deceptive and manipulative that they often become business leaders, CEOs, heads of charities or nonprofits, or wealthy wo/men with apparently "perfect" families... while being serial adulterers. They bounce off your honesty and authenticity, playing in your unconditional trusting and generous nature to perpetuate their master plan for domination. Not only are they incredibly cunning, deceptive, and manipulative, but they're also abusive, psychologically and emotionally violent, and fuelled by destruction. Chaos replaces peace, hate takes over authentic loving emotions, and false motives replace sincerity. Once you are enticed by the initial charm and charisma and under some belief or impression that they are genuine and warm hearted- nice people, capable of love, intimacy, friendship and companionship; it is very easy from this point to keep you trapped in their game.

5. Predator Vs Prey

Further, you are their prey, a vulnerable, open-hearted, genuine, loving, trusting, sensitive, empathic, naive, and innocent individual with a heart of gold. They are predators, emotional, psychological, spiritual, and physical predators. They know what they're doing too, so don't be fooled. How to tell you are truly an empath Vs being a narcissist? Your intentions are sincere. Your motivations are rooted in unity, loving kindness, selflessness, authentic service, and humility. You live with integrity, nobility, and a genuine need for community and cooperation. Narcissists see kindness, compassion, and so forth as weaknesses. They prey on your vulnerabilities, sensitivities, and need for authentic connection, romance, and emotional bonding. They are truly predators to a vulnerable and soft heart.

The Empath-Narcissist Dance or Karmic Entanglement

There is something known as the empath-narcissist dance or karmic entanglement with a narcissist. On your journey, you are bound to encounter at least one narcissist, but many of us encounter more. No, I'm not talking about someone a bit overly fiery and yang, nor am I referring to people who are extroverted, superficial, or a bit overzealous in their mannerisms and speech. I am talking about a real-life narcissist, someone sent to destroy your life. This may be a false lover, a parent, or a wolf in sheep's clothing, a friend, flatmate, or enemy masking as a friend. True narcissists, the ones with NPD, narcissism as a core personality blueprint, are life ruiners. They're sent here to test you, push you beyond your limits, and break you down so you can realize your worth... and your full potential. Narcissists who enter your life for more than a temporary bonding create a contract with you. This is an invisible contract, an energetic contract. It's also known as karmic entanglement, because you get wrapped up in their karma. You embark on a cycle of misery, suffering, and trauma, but there is a greater purpose; the mission is to rise up, become the most strong, beautiful, and self-empowered version of you, and rise up into stardom and personal victory.

You don't realize, at first, when you're in a relationship with a narcissist, but you do start to see the red flags and signs. It's an energetic dance, because you are their **fuel**. You are their ***narcissistic supply***. You become their primary fuel source, as you've given them your kindness, love, and energy. Through your unconditional trust, innocence, and love, you have entwined with them. From a higher, moreover timeless and cosmic perspective, you have created a soul contract with them. You're entered into a bond that is part of your soul's mission and ultimate journey here. This mission is to understand narcissism and its depths, so you can rise up, heal your traumas, both individual and ancestral, and find your worth, beauty, and talents. Without narcissists and their severe gaslighting, abuse, and emotional and psychological violence inflicted, you wouldn't be able to find your self-esteem or true abilities. Narcissists are the perfect weapon and ideal tool for healing and self-discovery in equal measure. You become a channel and soul guide for others to heal, as well as for planetary and collective consciousness. The pain and trauma you go through is not for nothing.

The stages of the empath-narcissist have already been described. But there's another thing to know and master, and this is in the connection this phenomena has to codependency. Due to your lack of boundaries coupled with your self-sacrificing nature, you can lack boundaries and therefore let in a lot of harmful energy. This makes you codependent, as first you trust, love, and give (over-give, I may add), and then you become codependent. With non-narcissists, this is still unhealthy, but it's not as dangerous. With narcissists, you are preyed on, through your naivety and innocence; the narcissist's intentions are not good, pure, or righteous. They are evil, twisted, and distorted, rooted in manipulation and a need to control you. Narcissists want to own you, entrapping you in their plots and schemes. Your life is a game to them, I'm sorry to say. **Fortunately**, you always have the choice to leave and end the vicious cycle of suffering. Regardless of how deep you get or how entwined your energies become, being with a narcissist in a romantic, platonic, or business partnership is always a transition. It is an opportunity to learn about yourself, heal, and evolve, growing and transforming like a butterfly from a cocoon.

Empath-Narcissist Dance recap, *Essential* info to learn and master:

- You are initially attracted to their charm, wisdom, and apparent (forced) kindness. They wow you with their affection, compliments, and charisma, and appear in a very positive social light.
- Their whole identity is entwined with appearing a positive light, and this means they have a strong social mask and facade. Everything they do and say is a con, but you don't know this... at the beginning.
- The relationship is defined by imbalance, selfishness, and manipulation. You are their fuel, their narcissistic supply. Narcissists are selfish and are primarily about what they can take. Reflect back on the story of Narcissus from Greek mythology. Similar to an energy vampire, they may drain you of your love, time, affection, resource, kindness, heart, spirit, and every atom of positivity you hold. It may only be a few weeks before their true intentions come to light.
- Due to such a strong level of control they have, it's impossible to break free, even at the early stages of the relationship. You are enticed, like a moth to a flame.

Their light is fake, but it feels so real to you. They steal your energy. They don't care that you have unraveled their mask, or witnessed their mindgames, plots, and manipulations.

- Pain, suffering, and perpetual heartbreak becomes the norm. This traumatic cycle can last months to years to decades; the end goal is to find your authentic voice, become the best version of yourself, and step into self-mastery.
- Finally, the whole experience is a con, an illusion... Like a princess trapped in the highest section of a tower awaiting her knight, an evil mastermind has put you there. It's a prison, a mental and psychological prison and sometimes a physical one. The illusion or fantasy is continued through your naivety combined with your unconditional trust and love. You hope, prey, and believe things will get better. You want so much to believe they are here to "save" you, to free you. Yet they are the ones keeping you bound and enslaved.
- It's saddening, it's heartbreaking, and it's soul-destroying, but it also makes you into *homo lumens*, the most breathtaking and awe-inspiring person, at the end of the dark tunnel.

Some other key points to reflect on:-

1. The love and depth you think they mirror back to you is an illusion. They are shallow, superficial, and only concerned with their own longevity and public image.
2. You may think they're your ideal reflection or perfect mirror; this is what a soulmate bond is supposed to be, right? Sorry, dear empath. It's not a soulmate bond, it's more like demonic possession.
3. The narcissist makes you question yourself, your intuition, your knowledge, and, over time, your own heart and values. Due to your love, moreover need for deep emotional connection, it can be hard to understand that the narcissist's shadow, wounds, and ways are not your own.

Your belief and truth that we are all a reflection of one another can leave you in a deep state of confusion and ultimately victimhood. Sacrifice, inner suffering, and the victim-martyr-savior complex can take over. *You become a martyr while trying to save a monster from their own dark fate.*

As you can see, this is not a healthy or happy connection. Yet when you are in that space and especially due to their initial charm, it can be very hard to get out of. Luckily the empath personality is strong and with such positive self-love and self-respect you will never choose to stay in this toxic relationship for too long a period of time. You may be drawn into the drama and toxicity for a short while, but you always come out of it much wiser, stronger, and intuitive, with your empathic qualities shining brightly.

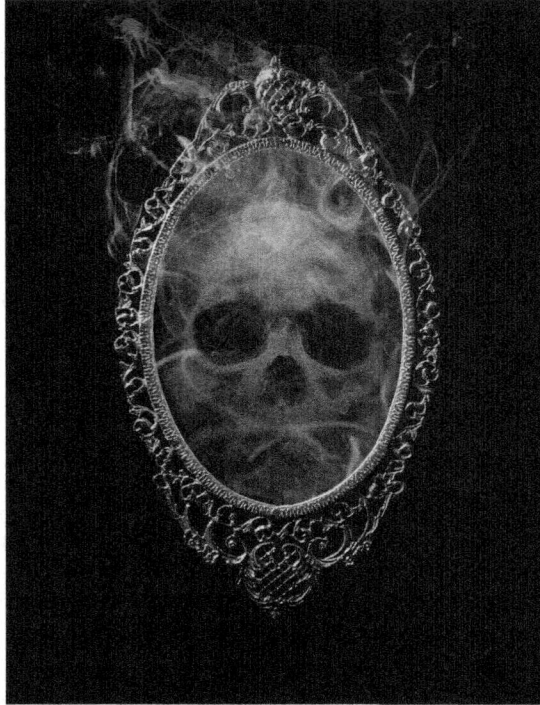

Specific Focus: Aspects of this Toxic-Dysfunctional Relationship

In a dysfunctional relationship you and your partner "bounce" off each other. Unfortunately, with a narcissist, it is extremely imbalanced, so this results in abuse. Verbal, emotional, or physical abuse combined with psychic attack- spiritual violence, ensue. Narcissistic abuse is common on the empath journey. Narcissists appear charming, friendly, kind, compassionate, and so on, and at the start of the bond you fall for it. This makes you attached, codependent, and always longing and hoping for their love. You have faith that things will get better, things will change, and that the dark spell is just a phase. It's not, however, it's their authentic self. Like Narcissus, the Greek river

God, narcissists entice you with their spells, their false flattery, fake kindness, and deceptive intentions. Daily interactions and energy exchanges turn into something monstrous quite early on. Let's explore real world scenarios now.

When you are empowered or aligned to your own path or soul mission

Quite simply, you're like catnip to a cat when you're aligned to your true purpose, life path, or destiny. Being self-empowered makes them want to take from you further. Feeling worthy, in high esteems, and full of beauty, talent, and positivity makes them want to squish you. They are energy vampires who feed off of your light, for real. Any passion, zest, soul spark, originality, creativity, or life force you have is theirs', by their demand and malicious, non-benevolent intent. You're like a bottle of cold, crystal clear water in front of someone who has been on a five hour hike, in the scorching sun. They *need* you and will or say anything to get to you. You are essentially a flame waiting to be put out.

When you are down or sensitive

You really start to see a narcissist's true evil and wicked colors when you're down and sensitive. Your lowest moments are when they shine... twisted, I know. Non-caring, lacking all compassion, sensitivity, kindness, and empathy, and completely barbaric and abusive, narcissists *love* to see you suffer. While you find joy from healing others, seeing animals receive love and comfort, or deep intimacy and companionship, their happiness, however fake, comes from your pain and suffering. Codependency's ultimate manifestation is when you are down or sensitive. A narcissist needs someone to attach to and they equally like to be clung on to, it amplifies their power. Once again, however false.

When talking about work

If you're someone who has a passion, vocation, or professional path and is immersed in it, quite happy and in a good place in life, before meeting your narcissist, it will be impossible to keep up your joy while with them. I am sorry to share, you will have to reduce your light, feel less passionate, and even feel a lot of dissatisfaction around your job. This is true even if you have the BEST job, career, or life path. Narcissists need you to feel low, depressed, and sad. They thrive off of your low self-worth and self-esteem, and further actively seek to diminish your happiness. When talking about work, you will need to dim your light, even put it out entirely. You have to play small, pretend like you're nothing, and act worthless. Your narcissistic partner will dismiss your abilities, talents, and successes entirely. They don't support you or care about you. What would usually be provided by a normal, loving, and caring partner is not given by the narcissist; they don't feel happy for you, they don't support you, and they don't possess any kind, listening, or considerate qualities. It's all about them, so your work suffers. Narcissists get annoyed, irritated, and upset by your successes. There's no joy for you, moreover they actually feel comfort in your pain.

There is such a strong level of gaslighting, using manipulative and abusive words and speech to make you appear crazy, that they will try to make you believe you're delusional. Real qualifications, titles, achievements, successes, and realities are dismissed and ridiculed. The narcissist won't accept or admit that they may not be real, that they're superficial, or that their entire identity is built off a facade (false charm, fake words and speech, superficiality, etc.). In worse cases, you may actually be made, forced, or coerced to quit your job altogether. Or turn down clients, miss important opportunities, or hide away in your home being reclusive and cut off from the world. It's a painful and vicious cycle, dating or being married to a narcissist. Cold indifference, nastiness, or a condescending and superior attitude is all you're met with. Alternatively, you're shouted at, ridiculed, or "put in your place" with clear words and body language that says, 'you're nothing.' Narcissists are different species of human, dear empath. This is something you must come to terms with if you wish to heal and break free.

What normal people find deeply embarrassing, disturbing, and intolerable due to a complete lack of compassion and human kindness, narcissists thrive off of. In terms of your life path, career, or service, narcissists need you to dim, down, or diminish your light so they can feel high and mighty. The entire narcissist identity is a facade, a fake and superficial front, and a mask. So, your authenticity unveils their mask. This is why empaths can't have a real job, be successful, or speak about their professional projects or victories. All passion must go out of the window when with a narcissist. Below are some questions will you start to ask yourself:

"How could I possibly let someone so indifferent, cold, and selfish into my personal space?"

"I thought we were on the same wavelength, where did I go wrong?"

"I truly believed s/he was sincere, charming, and beautiful. What on earth is going on?!"

The gaslighting tactics are so strong that you begin to question reality. A perfect example: You could literally be holding a certificate produced by a recognized body/establishment in your hand, after a year long training course, and the narcissist will look you in the eyes and tell you it's not real. Then, they continue to hammer into your psyche the belief that it's not real, and that you even attended the training... through abuse, gaslighting, and severe manipulation tactics.

On this note, it's important to consider that this is why those experienced in this field will always tell you that narcissists are a whole new breed of human; they're *not* human. They're so heartless, cruel, and inhuman that they can be referred to as diabolical (demonic), at least when compared to the empath personality.

When with friends or family

One of the most brutal aspects of being in a relationship or bond of any kind with a narcissist is how they speak and act around your friends. Your friends and family, who are supposed to be your biggest supporters, your confidants, and your gems and jewels to rely on, become their biggest fans and followers. Unconsciously. How do they achieve this? Through advanced repetition of false stories and ideas. The narcissist will lie about you on repeat and then convince everyone these lies are true. You may be thinking, this isn't that dangerous, but you're wrong. Over time, the level of support you receive from apparent friends and family diminishes, and when you're at the final stages, ready to break free from the narcissist, the support you need isn't there. Narcissists can convince someone white is black while black is white. Your narcissistic parent, partner, or lover will turn everyone against you, and at brutal levels. They make people laugh at your suffering, think you're just being dramatic, or twist and distort reality at severe levels. When it's finally time for you to muster the courage to leave, which is quite difficult for your sweet and fragile heart, which has further already been abused and battered many, many times, the support systems you need aren't there. People think you're delusional. Or crazy. Or in need of therapy.

Your own friends and family believe you've been lying or distorting the truth, when really it's the other way round. This is how powerful narcissists' words and malicious intentions are. They deliver their plots and schemes with such clarity and conviction that even a judge would believe their false stories. This is also why it's advised to never bring emotions and feelings into a court case, if you were to ever take them to court (for matters of money, children, or shared resources). Stick to facts and figures only because their entire identity is wrapped around heavy emotional manipulation and gaslighting. Thus, all support is removed from your life. You are seen as weak, why, rude, crazy, in need of therapy, or simply a liar. The reality is, the narcissist is all of these things, hence narcissistic abuse being intrinsically connected to the term *gaslighting*. Being with a narcissistic partner is a very difficult and painful thing. At home, alone with them, it's constant bullying, belittling, and slander or verbal/emotional abuse. When in public, you're not allowed to speak, unless your words support their campaign. You are either a direct victim or if you choose a path of attempting to rise above victimhood, you are the sufferer in the relationship. You have to go through endless attempts of lifting your partner up, helping them see the light, and putting the energy into showing them a better way. You find yourself exhibiting vast levels of compassion, patience, kindness and empathy, which all take a lot of energy from you. Yet, when you are around friends and family nothing is wrong! They are the life and soul of the gathering, charming, warm-hearted, gregarious, wise, and so forth. Behind closed doors you're bullied and belittled at extreme levels, but in public all is well, apparently. Your feelings are treated like a yo-yo. You are treated like their plaything or toy.

In terms of being finally ready to break free, the support you need is gone because your friends and family believe you've been lying or exaggerating the truth. This leaves you alone and victimized. If you try to expose the truth in front of others, in a social setting? The narcissist is the type of person who would punch a young woman in the face or gut and make everyone believe you stabbed them (with a knife) behind closed doors. It's a very dark and demonic energy to embody. They make up the most elaborate stories, perpetuate false ideas, and reinforce their plots and mind games so that you are created to be the most crazy, deranged, and deluded or evil person. Of course, it's all the other way around... A true narcissist's energy is so dark that your own family could watch you get punched, physically assaulted, and reduced to tears- clearly a helpless victim in need of serious support (to evolved empaths and anyone with their intuition intact) and think it's justified. *"My empath sister/daughter/friend clearly deserves this in some way."* It's f*cked up. And this is why I do use the word demonic when explaining narcissistic abuse and its effect on empaths. Furthermore, there will always be someone in your family who you are closest to, and, I am so sorry to share, but this person will be their closest confidant. It's a heartbreaking experience, however it will only make you stronger and more aligned to your true path, purpose, and soul mission in this life.

Charm, humor, false compliments and flattery, a colorful and positive personality, warmth, and apparent wisdom and power are how the narcissist entices you, your friends, and your family. So look out for these signs/red flags at the beginning.

> The best thing you can do to regain support is to sit down with the person you feel you wish to confide in. You need to make sure that they know you are being serious and are in need of a real heart to heart. Anything less than complete depth, honesty, and vulnerability, coupled with a bearing of your soul, and you won't find the level of awareness and perception you need. Make sure you are first serious with yourself before opening up to someone.

When in social settings

Social settings feed the illusions and false motives of the narcissist. A narcissist's entire identity is wrapped around their social facade and mask, which means they've done a lot of work to gain admirers, fans, and followers! They need constant attention, despite appearing to have it all together. They need reinforcers in the same way they rely on your friends and family to reinforce their manipulative agendas when you're finally ready to spill the truth (of their abuse). They live to cheat, deceive, and take the spotlight. No-one else is allowed in the spotlight. No-one else is allowed to be as talented, brilliant, beautiful, shiny, or successful as them. It's their world, but not in a natural or organic way like in those who live with heart (*you are the center of your universe*). Unlike slightly egotistical or self-centered people, everyone is expendable. People are commodities, tools for their glory and social facade. Narcissists step over people, use others, and expect complete loyalty to reinforce their stories and fake charm. They may choose one or two people they actually consider "friend," a real friend, but they'll never have real connections with authentic emotions and depth with others. It's all done on a superficial level. When it comes to those few groundbreaking moments in social scenarios where you really and truly need a partner, a soulmate, and a best friend; well, good luck getting it from a narcissist.

When alone

When you are alone together this is where the true signs of a dysfunctional relationship come out. It is virtually impossible for a narcissist to hide their true colors when alone with you, one-to-one; you are trapped in an endless cycle of giving and taking, yet this giving and taking is not balanced nor is it just. Let's look at the characteristics of the giving (solely empath) taking (solely narcissist) cycles present in this relationship.

- You recognize something is not right and start to see the narcissist's shadow. Because you truly love them, moreover want to see the relationship work, you begin a cyclic routine of offering compassion, patience, and love. You go the extra mile to give them what they need, always putting them first, as this is your natural way.
- You try to make them see sense through attempting to bring them up to your frequency. You may occasionally do moments of the opposite, attempting to 'match their vibe' and resort to brief frustration, anger, impatience, intolerance, or unkindness. In a normal relationship these tactics may work as you realize everyone is capable of compassion, further admitting when they are wrong and returning to the light. Yet in a relationship with a narcissist all of your efforts and intentions go to waste- there's no reasoning with your partner.
- You constantly feel like you have to dim your light for your partner. You simply are not allowed to shine, be successful, achieve anything above and beyond your relationship, or actively show and experience personal joy and satisfaction in *any* way. Your partner's ego suppresses you every time. Their ego overpowers your light, and personal and professional relationships suffer as a result.
- If you are already committed to some self-love, self-care, or healing practice, the only times you feel truly content and free to be yourself is when you have distanced yourself and are doing your own thing. Going for a walk in nature, immersing yourself in some project or hobby outside of your home, creative cooking, enjoying your fave pastimes, and taking sufficient time to be with friends or family are not allowed or only allowed in small amounts. Being in a relationship with a narcissist drains you, it drains you of everything you have.
- The attention is *always* on them. They are selfish, egotistical, and self-righteous; self-entitled, mean-spirited, destructive, abusive, and insensitive. You are their target, fuel, and supply in one. Your beauty, compassion, empathy, selflessness, and angelic superhuman qualities are wasted on them. While you're sincere,

they're a gameplayer. While you strive for authentic bonding, they can only meet on a very superficial and shallow, surface level.

- Finally, absolutely anything you do, say, or believe is met with complete resistance. You say white so they say black. You shine light, so they express shadow. Compromise, balance, and harmony... cooperation, mutual respect, and fairness... non-existent! Further, you are manipulated to feel that you are always wrong, crazy, or stupid. You are treated like a doormat, dustbin, and projection wall. There is light at the end of the tunnel, however.

In the bedroom

Sexually, romantically, and intimately being with a narcissist is not something one would advise once "in the know" about narcissism and its dirty secrets. The 'empath-narcissist dance' is amplified in the bedroom, and this can make a dark experience. Dom-sub dynamics are amplified and played out, always at expense to you. Remember the duality symbol. Empaths are feminine, passive, and submissive. Narcissists are masculine, forceful, and dominant. Unfortunately, you become their personal plaything. You're their toy, their sex toy at worst, but definitely their emotional dumping ground. They unload all of the toxic vibrations of their own games and manipulations onto you. Take your awareness back to when you first met. They were charming, wise, funny, lovable, attentive to your needs, sexy, and highly attractive. *This is the persona they exhibit to get their needs met.* Exhibit is not the accurate term to use: force, push, trick, manipulate, and execute with utmost dominance and intensity would all be more accurate. In short, you are magnetized to their manipulations while holding onto the memories of how things used to be, right at the beginning. Narcissists aren't capable of real love, devotion, or loyalty.

They're serious adulterers and players. They use you in the bedroom. They play on your feelings, moreover your need for something real and authentic. They will convince you something not real is real (their loyalty and whereabouts or feelings and emotions) and something real is not real (their cheating, dishonesty, etc.) The games of a narcissist in the bedroom are more psychological, mental, and emotional. They know- at least intellectually- that desire, bond, love, intimacy, and emotional, mental and psychological merging are natural and healthy, so they play on this. They receive great pleasure from your silent suffering and bring out the gaslighting tactics when you start to sense them cheating or using manipulation tactics. In terms of the dom-sub relationship, it can be very thrilling at first. But ultimately this is a dangerous, dysfunctional, and unhealthy bond rooted in (extremely) imbalanced dynamics.

"The Narcissist's Poem"- *Inside the Mind of A Narcissist...*

You can find the spoken word version *here*: (Link below.[1])

I like to make you feel weak, small, and worthless,
I constantly ingrain the belief that you're not worthy of abundance.
Through criticism, blackmail, emotional abuse, and mental confusion-
I hammer into your psyche endless chaos and confusion... illusion.

I convince you you're not worthy of love, I ruin your self-esteem,
I bully you on repeat then remain in the Unseen.
Around friends, family, peers, and social & friendship and connection groups;
I can convince them that you're shy and rude.

This is my tool, you know, my secret chosen weapon-
I constantly play on your kindness and authentic need for connection.
I choose sensitive and generous souls as my target,
as I am fully aware that they keep giving, their identity is rooted in kindness.

I am a bully, an oppressor, an abuser and a liar,
I am full of BS, totally manipulative, and insult, ridicule, and slander.
I can make others think white is black, while black is white,
while behind closed doors my nastiness keeps you awake every night.

My sole intention is to destroy your spirit, to keep you small and weak...
I seek power, status, recognition, attention- without humility.
I am totally self-serving, self-entitled and arrogant,
Selfish, undermining and full of hypocrisy and intimidating actions.

I set and live by different standards- I am allowed to be free in every moment,
to be the mean-spirited, deceptive, and hurtful ugly tyrant!
Yet you, the genuine one with a gentle and compassionate spirit
are abused to the point of starting to believe life is not even worth living.

I gaslight you, I turn your whole world upside down, then I make you appear
crazy...

---

[1] https://www.youtube.com/watch?v=FFT1m-aFn4g&t=6s

Delusional, irrational, ungrounded or in need of therapy;
when *my* personality is rooted in manipulation and insanity,
in knowing full well I'm a narcissist who perpetually distorts reality.

When it's at the point where you're in constant darkness and despair,
and when people are afraid to speak up even when they know it's not right or fair,
Because I am a REAL bully, a toxic & sociopathic tyrant,
I lack humility, selflessness, and grace- and act and take whatever I want...

I then laugh- I lighten up the situation with my positive charm and fake flattery,
Behind closed doors I psychologically and emotionally abuse you, yet to others I am sanity!
I know how to make others see me as a boss, someone with real success and talent,
Yet this confidence is built on putting others down, making up stories, and causing havoc.

I cause chaos, destruction, ill-wishes, and do some downright psychotic sh*t
then I make YOU out to be the pathetic and mean-spirited "d*ck" or "b*tch!"
The truth is, you were only ever kind and genuine to me- you treated me with the love all humans want.
And now I've turned your friends & family against you, no-one believes you're the Chosen One.

"Oh, I am just this sweetly charming and successful winner,"
No, you idiot, I am a loser,
I just threw the real winner under the bus,
Distorting perception and hiding the truth so you believed my victim wasn't full of love...

And while you were sat there by my side shaming them and joining in on the "fun,"
You were lowering yourself to my evil level, not realizing that it all can never be undone.
See, I need my circle of followers- I desire nothing more than to be admired.
I need to be seen as mighty & strong, because behind the scenes I am really powerless.

I am powerless.

I have no talent, I have no gifts; my charm and confidence are all a lie,
They're built off the hard work and fame of others, the people I cause hell to so my true self can hide.
It's all a joke to me too, and at the start and end of each day,
I won't really care about you either... you're just a pawn in the way I play.

It's all my way, my way, my way, and if anyone tries to get in the way;
I cheat, play dirty, use tricks and pure f*ckery, and make sure everyone submits to my game.
Did you speak out? Did you try to expose me? Did you try to bring the truth to light?!
Now you're screwed, as I will literally destroy your life!

I'll make up stories that never happened and present them as true...
I will, quite literally, type up messages birthed from my mean-spiritedness and present them as you.
I will sue you, report you, steal and cheat- I will try to take your security and livelihood,
and then sit there projecting my sh*t, denying all accountability and responsibility.

That's the thing, sweet and sincere- normal and sane, people;
I never admit to my games of manipulation,
I have no sense of real humility, fairness, justice, or honest communication.
All I care about is my own victory and survival, my social facade and false intentions.

My sole desire is people believing my BS and lies,
I don't care if it comes in the way of a family bond, true love, and something divine.
Again, I lack sensitivity, authenticity, and I am incapable of compassion and empathy...
Kindness is weakness while heart-centered vibrations are a myth- I see it all as a ridiculous fantasy.

So, here is my message to you, healthy and healed people of light,

Next time you encounter me, stop appeasing me for an easy life.
I am not ok, I am not normal- I actually have a mental health condition,
NPD is a disorder, a severe distortion creating immense separation.

Put up some boundaries, simply walk away, and don't submit to my false wit and charm;
Know that my social facade is literally a mask, a way to keep me causing illness and harm.
Stand strong in your light, never start to see empathy and kindness as something to shame,
as these two qualities alone keep me living in delusion and the insane.

Learn how to deal with a true narcissist in the right way, because we can be incredibly vengeful.
Anyone who tries to expose us brings out rage and pure inner venom.
We are toxic, insensitive, mean-spirited, abusive and totally low vibrational,
So be self-loving and self-respecting while equally protecting your sacred vessel.

And if you were one of my fans and followers who I totally consciously deceived (yippee for me!),
Remember to *say sorry* to the one I sought to destroy, your once loyal friend or kin- your family.
Don't stay on my wavelength thinking you have a real friend or lover in me,
I really don't care about you, I am a selfish, a gaslighting narcissist- yet there are people that need an apology.

Seriously, listen to my message, this coming from my soul- the only truth you will ever get.
Listen to your gut feelings and intuitive hunches, and make peace with your part in the bullsh*t.
Because the chances are I made you turn against one of the most sincere and loving souls...
One of the rare gems who are selfless, and really do care about the world and whole.

If you're the one I abused and targeted, well- sucks to be you, you fool!
Even when you're clearly winning, healed, and free of me I will only ever see you as a stool,

to my self-deception, destruction, insecurity- my uncontrollable desire to maintain my Mask;
No matter where you go in life you will always be the enemy, the one I slander & ridicule when I need a laugh.

◇

Chapter 3: Empath Evolved... Self-Mastery

Turning Sensitivity Into A Superpower

In this section, we will be looking at what it means to be an *introverted empath* and *an extroverted empath*, in addition to how they overlap. An introverted empath embodies the qualities of an introvert. These qualities are an aversion to big groups, loud social gatherings, and superficial scenarios. A preference is given to one-to-one or small group interactions, and you thrive in deep and meaningful conversations with 1- 5 people max. You find real joy and inner contentment in solitude and solo activities. You're deeply imaginative, creative, and artistic, with a powerful intuition. Psychic and extrasensory powers flow to you. You're spiritually receptive, wise, insightful, deep, and philosophical. Extroverts, on the other hand, thrive in social situations and receive their stimulation as such. They are confident, highly expressive, and lovers of small-talk, as well as superficial and shallow interactions. They like to gossip, be frivolous, and experience high enthusiasm and excitability over depth. Communication can be excessive to the point of dulling the mind. A love of drama, chaos, and a multitude of stimulation define extroverts.

When healed, on top form, and self-mastered, empaths are introverted-extroverts. This means you take all of your amazing qualities, strengths, and abilities, and apply them to being sociable. It's not that you don't like socializing, it's just that you're very selective. You also prefer stimulation, communication, and activities that add soul or sustenance to your life. You choose inspirational activities over instant gratification and drama, gossip, and distractions. You will always be sensitive, prone to introspection and mellowness, even within a social situation, and overly emotional, these are your shadow traits and are inescapable. As an empath, it may be clear that one of the best ways to heal and overcome your sensitivities is to embody some of the characteristics of an extrovert. This does not mean you have to compromise or sacrifice your true nature, it simply means that it may be worth your while to *balance and adapt,* so you are better able to exist in social situations. This is especially true if you find yourself taking on the more negative characteristics of an introvert, such as social anxiety, nervous tension, shyness, unhealthy humility- modesty at the expense of self, or self-esteem and confidence issues. Taking steps to be less introverted or introspective can help you develop mental strength, clarity, and tenacity, strengthening your psychological muscle. Self-alignment, personal growth, and unification of masculine and feminine attributes are also possible.

This is not suggesting you should start shouting, being rude or aggressive, or forcing yourself to play a role you're not comfortable with. Yang qualities, which are generally symbolic of extroversion, are also innovative, upbeat, optimistic, colorful, passionate, and joyous- qualities core to your true passions and nature. You may struggle with assertiveness, being direct, and dominance, also yang qualities, but they are not the only ones. To step into self-leadership for any personal or professional role, it's essential to get familiar with the characteristics of extroversion. You can learn from your 'yang' friends too, finding guidance and wisdom in the people you would normally teach or heal, when in your "holding space," caregiver, counselor, healer, or therapist self. Being more masculine, yang or extroverted can help you overcome social anxiety, mental confusion, and apathy, as well as hyper-emotionalism, nervous tension, or an overactive mind. As a psychic sponge, you pick up on a lot, but receiving multiple impressions, thoughts, and emotions all the time is not healthy. This only occurs when you're fully in your empath self, connected to your powerful instincts, intuition, and driving force to help and serve. Aiming to be more extroverted can help you to integrate your intellectual, logical, and cerebral side.

Truth Is In the Food: EMPATH DIET ESSENTIALS!

No matter your path, chosen profession, or desired modes of service, diet is very important to the empathic constitution. Regardless of your ethnicity, heritage, astrological make-up, gender, or numerology, all empaths are sensitive. Emotions and feelings fuel you, and this means taking care of your physical health. A healthy body is a healthy mind and spirit. From my own journey and copious research, here are the best foods I can recommend for the empath nature. I am not a nutritionist, but I do hold a diploma in Herbalism. I've also studied this in depth.

It has already been established that you have a healing nature, thus a huge part of being an empath lies within your healing capabilities. Many empaths go on to become intuitive healers, therapists, psychics, physicians, or spiritual counselors and teachers. Many empaths make amazing astrologers, nurses, caregivers, or animal communicators. Are you a musician or artist? You will need to take care of your health too! All foods contain life force, vibrations. The foods you eat and lifestyle choices you make determine how much light, compassion, and empathy you hold. Clean and healthy eating is essential for your empathic destiny.

1. Raw Living Food

Any raw living food is ideal for you. This includes sprouts and sprouting vegetables, kimchi, and other home-made or ethically sourced living foods. Living foods contain the highest amount of natural enzymes- enzymes that help to remove toxins from the body. Raw living foods are high in life force, they haven't been polluted or diminished with chemicals and so on. They assist you in establishing a deep connection to the natural world, which increases self-esteem, personal power and sovereignty, happiness, well-being, and overall mood! Raw living foods allow you to function at a high emotional frequency, moreover maintain your spiritual vibration and life force.

2. Leafy Greens

Dark leafy greens raise your vibration, truth be told. They are very high in life force, nutrition content, and water, so they keep you feeling full while equally feeling "light." Any food that comes closer to source, aka 'primary' food types, contain very powerful levels of chi. Chi is essential for health, vitality, and well-being. Of course, this keeps you strong and physically able, which allows you to develop and maintain healthy boundaries. They also keep your mind strong, clear, and energized, so you can keep your mind, body, & spirit system functioning at a high level. *Leafy greens include*: Spinach, lettuce, collard greens, arugula (rocket), chard, broccoli, mustard greens, and kale.

3. Avocados

One of the best healthy protein and fat sources for vegetarians, vegans, and those choosing to go plant-based, avocados should be a staple to your diet, dear empath. Avocados are loaded with healthy and nutritious nutrients, vitamins, and minerals, as well as monounsaturated fats (the healthy kind of fat). They have a lot of antioxidants, which contribute to many bodily functions, including eye and heart health. As you may notice, there are no "meats" included in this empath diet essentials list. This is because of the intrinsic connection eating animals has to emotional and spiritual awareness and connection, or, more specifically, disconnection. Your cells "'know" and are deeply intelligent, consciousness flows through your veins and your cells just as it streams through your mind and the waters of a river. In the natural world, animals contribute to the rivers and oceans and ecosystems- we're not functioning off some predatory "nature consumes all life" paradigm-mindset-reality. In other words, animals are a secondary or even tertiary food source that we don't need to consume. We *don't* need animals for protein, and it's certainly not compassionate or empathic to eat animals simply for taste. Humans, nature, and animals are supposed to live in harmony. The empathic constitution is suited to a high vibrational vegetarian, consciously vegan, or plant-based diet.

4. Walnuts

All nuts are excellent for you, but one particular one I'd like to highlight is walnuts. Walnuts are the ultimate brain nut for empaths who may need a bit more wit, intellect, and psychological strength. They increase assertiveness, and direct communication, in addition to calming and soothing the neurological pathways that are required for a balanced and serene mindset. Walnuts have one of the highest antioxidant compositions of all the nuts, thus they eliminate stress, which can help with putting up clear boundaries against toxic and narcissistic characters. They help to keep your watery-emotional qualities aligned and strong; they have an incredible effect on your brain and therefore psychological and mental well being, which intrinsically influences your emotions, and intuitive and spiritual powers...

5. Superfood Smoothies and Supplements

Superfood smoothies and supplements in the form of herbal remedies (powders, pills, etc.) are one of the best ways to keep your emotional, psychological, physical, and spiritual health up to par. The best kinds of milk to use are organic and natural nut or dairy-free milks, like hemp, almond, cashew, hazelnut, coconut, or soy milk. These can be mixed with a variety of fruits and superfoods, including *Chlorella, spirulina, wheatgrass, lucuma, baobab,* and *moringa* (and *maca*). They are all high in life force, nutrients, and energy, moreover amplify a strong and powerful connection to nature, Source, and the divine. They aid in emotional connection and awareness.

6. Maca

Maca is a superfood found in Peru that provides energy, vitality, and potent healing vibrations. It is known to increase sexual vitality and libido, which can be very beneficial for overcoming emotional eating, bloating, heaviness, and depressive or antisocial thoughts and feelings. Overeating is associated with the empath nature because you feel things so deeply. You become burdened with everyone's problems and emotions in a way that limits, blocks, and suppresses you. You "take on" everyone else's sh*t, in other words, and this can make you look and feel heavier than what you actually are. I believe some haters called me obese once when I was a curvy size 14 because I started to uncover some truths about their narcissistic tendencies... As an empath's entire identity is rooted in emotional connection and oneness, we can make ourselves appear heavier or bigger than we actually are. This all begins on a spiritual, psychological, or emotional level. Maca is amazing for calming, balancing, and stabilizing emotions, mood swings, and melancholy or sadness linked to feeling so much. It can help increase social warmth and friendliness, sexual vitality, and genuine desires for intimacy and connection. You can buy maca as pills or superfood powder for smoothies or salads.

7. Superfruits

All fruits are ideal, as they contain high water content, with water being the source of life. Simply put, they help you thrive emotionally, spiritually, psychologically, and physically. Superfruits include strawberries, raspberries, blueberries, goji berries, goldenberries, gooseberries, cranberries, and any other berry you come across. They connect you to the natural world and a natural vibration, and are simultaneously high in universal life force energy. They enhance purity while aiding in your intuitive and creative abilities. Water symbolizes the subconscious mind, astral wisdom, sacred knowledge, the imagination, divine truths and inspiration, creative genius, artistic gifts, instincts, emotional intelligence, intuition, and psychic and spiritual abilities... All of these are amplified with superfruits and berries! *Interesting fact*: There are people who live off fruits alone, these people are called *fruitarians*. Although I am not suggesting you become one, fruitarians are some of the happiest and healthiest people alive. And if anyone could achieve this, it would be a superhuman empath.

8. Cacao

Another empath essential, cacao is also known as raw chocolate and is extremely good for emotional issues or imbalances. Cacao is rich in antioxidants, high in nutrients, and holistically makes you feel good. It releases happy endorphins while stimulating spiritual gifts and powers. Cacao creates a deep bond with Mother Earth, ancestral energies, and ancient wisdom and knowledge that can keep you aligned to your true path and purpose. A fun thing to know and explore is that when you drink cacao, either in a smoothie or as a hot chocolate, the plant leaves *a trail* on the side of your glass; it *looks like roots*! The truth is, cacao is a beautiful and sacred plant that has only been polluted (with chemicals, artificial hormone-infused dairy milk, and other intoxicants) in the modern age. Cacao has been used and consumed for thousands of years, by many ancient, shamanic, and spiritually in tune cultures and communities. Cacao activates your Third Eye, inner spirit, and divine body. You can drink it, make it into chocolate, or use it in ceremonies for Heart chakra activation.

9. Medicinal Mushrooms

One of the most powerful foods high in life force and water content, yet simultaneously spiritually connecting, are medicinal mushrooms. These include *Reishi, Oyster, Shitake, Maitake, Lions Mane, Cordyceps*, and *Chaga* and can be consumed as a tea, eaten, or taken as supplements. Medicinal mushrooms connect you to higher and evolved consciousness, while activating lots of hidden gifts.

10. Organic and Wholefoods

Any organic or wholefood, a food source that has come straight from the earth, are perfect for your heightened emotions, spiritual awareness, and sensitivities. When you are looking to make a life-long change, moreover heal from emotional related issues for good, it is very important that you keep in mind your holistic self. A diet is not just a short term fix, a diet is a lifestyle. Wholefoods include beans, pulses, legumes, vegetables, nuts, and seeds. Fish, lean meats, and seafood are much better meat choices than red meat, or meat which has been processed in a commercialized way. (If you're not ready to make the change to vegetarian or plant-based.) Factory farms coupled with a lot of the meat sold in Western society has many detrimental health effects, least to mention the sentient creatures who have given their lives for our "protein" are thrown away in the trash. Organic and wholefood, plant-based foods, are much healthier, compassionate, and empathic-supportive choices.

11. Purified, Clean, and Mineral Water

Although it is not food, pure and clean water should arguably be included. Drinking lots of water is essential for all the reasons, qualities, and gifts explored so far. Your water should be: purified, mineral, mountain, natural, filtered if you have no other option, or reverse osmosis. You can also make your own crystal water, with the healing powers and qualities of the crystals removing impurities and psychic debris (negative energy) from the water. Water cleanses, purifies, and activates your mind, body, and spirit system, as well as your creative, soul-aligned, and spiritual gifts. You might want to consider regular fasts too. Just a 3-day water fast cleanses and detoxes the liver; a 7-day water fast can begin cell regeneration, kick-starting your entire immune system. Besides fasting, water is life force at its purest, as it is the water element that can provide you with fine-tuned intuition and sensitivity. If you are ever suffering from heavy emotions or low moods, water can be a game changer!

Food Sources and Chi: "Low Vibed" Vs "High Vibed" Foods

To be enlightened is to be aware, intuitive, insightful, Higher Self activated, and connected to your own source of spiritual power and knowing. It also means being connected to your body, both the physical body that holds you and the planet that sustains you. Enlightenment inherently involves feelings of *lightness,* which cannot be achieved when you are feeling heavy or bloated from everyone's pains and hardships. Remember: not all weight is physical. Empaths hold onto emotional weight, making you look bigger, heavier, and unhealthier than you actually are. An empath can project the image of someone fat, bloated, or spaced out and mental in society's eyes, when they have taken on too much, are living in apathy and disassociation, or feel they need to protect themselves from the outside world. In this respect there is a deep connection between confidence, self-esteem, and being empowered and diet. Truth is in the food, food is energy. What energy are you feeding yourself with? Low vibrational foods disconnect you, keep you in a state of suffering, and cut you off from your empathic gifts. High vibed foods do the opposite. Connected to this topic is the aspect of primary, secondary, and tertiary foods, which is linked to both compassionate morals and physical health ideals.

Chi is the term used to describe the *universal life force energy* that flows through every living thing. It is in the fruits and vegetables we eat, animals, the sun, sea, air, and lands of the world. Chi is invisible, but very real. Martial artists, for example, have been aware of chi and its power for thousands of years. Some of the greatest martial artists and kung fu masters get their power, moreover their unique abilities solely from their awareness and cultivation of chi. Chi is diminished in foods full of artificial chemicals and preservatives, or foods high in fats or carbohydrates. Below are some examples of high vibrational foods.

Food with high life force/chi:-

- Fruits, vegetables, nuts, and seeds.
- Pulses, beans, legumes, and grains.
- Organic and whole foods.
- Natural oils like hemp, coconut, flaxseed, avocado, and olive.
- Herbs and herbal supplements.
- Plant-based, mostly organic vegan foods (non-processed).

The 'Primary' & 'Secondary' Cycles

Something that isn't hugely well known are the primary and secondary cycles. This is referring to the amount of chi, direct source energy, in food. Outside of veganism and vegetarianism chosen for moral, spiritual, and heart-centered reasons, this topic is great to know for physical well-being and longevity. When we eat organic wholefoods that have come directly from the earth, the food source is in its primary cycle. In other words, the nutrients, vitamins and feel good natural chemicals have come directly from the air, sun, earth and rain. They can be seen to have the *highest levels of chi*. Most animals, if we choose to eat them, are in their secondary cycle, they receive their energy from eating crops. Once we consume the animals, therefore, a lot of the nutrients and essentials from plant-based food sources have already been digested (and metabolized). This means that we have wasted a life, a sentient creature (an animal) to not actually receive the nutrients or chi we require! Barbaric, ludicrous, or insane, you may be thinking? This is why many empaths go vegan. Of course, eating animals who are carnivores then makes our food source tertiary; the food we consume to sustain us has gone through yet *another* cycle.

In essence, choosing a diet that has come solely from the elements of nature means the best possible vibration for ourselves. All of life can be seen to be measured in terms of vibration, frequency, and energy, so consuming food that's suffered extensive trauma, pain, and suffering ultimately means we absorb these frequencies. Animals suffer, experience supreme fear, anxiety, trauma, pain, and heartache before they're murdered. This transmits into their cells before death, which we then eat. This means their trauma, pain, and fear merges with our cells and subtle energy bodies. It creates a karmic cycle, It perpetuates violence and injustice. Ultimately, it disconnects us from our best empathic, compassionate, and sensitive-nurturing gifts. The vibration and frequency of the food passes on to us, not only physically, but spiritually, energetically, and on a quantum and holographic plane. Choosing primary food sources has so many wonderful benefits, for your mind, body, emotions, spirit, and soul, in this life and future ones.

Self-Leadership: An Essential 'Masculine Trait' to Embody

As an empath, you project an aura that screams, "come and unload all your sh*t onto me! I will be your emotional dumping ground." That's when your boundaries are weak. You're brilliant, beautiful, wise, genuine, and multi-talented, you're an amazing soul. You have a heart of gold. But until you learn how to protect your energy, your aura tells people it's ok to abuse you, subtly or viciously, indirectly or directly. Being so feminine, passive, and unconditionally loving, can be a degrading experience. Your key to success is to practice self-leadership, and with this comes self-respect, self-love, self-alignment, self-sovereignty, and self-empowerment. As a selfless being who is prone to self-sacrifice, it's important to get clear on your "self," i.e. your psyche, personality, and core soul programming. Your auric field can be a protective and supportive bubble that speaks of wonder, magic, and love. Or it can be a breeding ground for chaos and destruction. Illusions and confusions seep through when you fail to recognize and honor your needs, self-care, and healthy self-love and healing measures. Your aura perpetually transmits, receives, and interacts with subtle-spiritual energy, moreover "converses" with multiple frequencies and energies around you. Your aura picks up on multiple thoughts, emotions, beliefs, intentions, and impressions. When you have weak boundaries, you pick up on negativity and darkness. When you have strong boundaries, you pick up on light, angelic, and higher consciousness or unified energy currents.

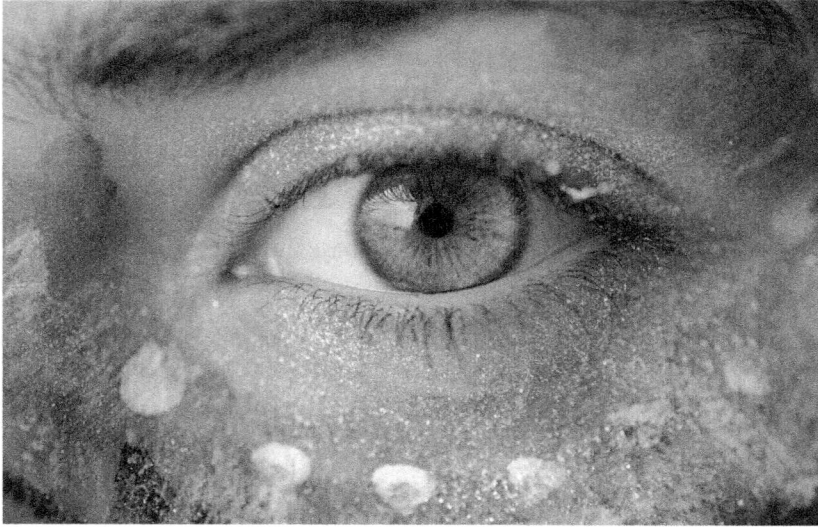

Because you see the world in a compassionate, caring, and empathic way and unconsciously take on the role of the healer, counselor, and caregiver, you can become an emotional dumping ground, everyone's doormat, and a victim or recipient of narcissistic abuse. Until you get to the autonomous, self- sovereign, and independent stage you are likely codependent in some way. One key quality not yet explored that you must find some synergy with is discernment. When I made my first video on narcissism on my youtube channel, the *Dream & Spirit Weaver*, I couldn't even pronounce the word! I said it incorrectly, without the silent 'c,' and this was because I hadn't yet perfected the quality. Without discernment, you can't give wise counsel, nor do you possess sound judgment. Discernment is a combination of logic and intuition, higher analytical reasoning and instincts, and mental gifts and emotional sensitivity, intelligence, and vulnerability. To discern is to judge, but in a sensitive, healthy, and insightful way. In this respect, it can be seen that you often *lack judgment* and thus unconsciously open yourself up to unwanted energies.

Remember how this manifests: a stranger's shoulder to cry on, a lack of grounding and stability in your life, impracticalities with money and finances, irresponsibilities, an emotional dumping ground, a doormat, a narcissist or energy vampire magnet, and minor to major energy depletion. Unwanted energies are what prevent you from stepping into self-leadership, because you're always getting absorbed in the false stories, motives, and dramas of others. With discernment and self-leadership, you become a powerful wayshower, changemaker, and healer or visionary, stepping into greatness and self-mastery.

Empath Sexuality

Exploring your sexuality is one major part of your healing journey back to wholeness, harmony, and integration. Romantic and intimate sexual relationships tend to involve adequate amounts of pain and suffering early in life, as we as empaths tend to attract narcissists, abusers, and energy vampires into our auric field. We also attract oppressors, users, and people who take advantage of our gentle nature. As we're naturally submissive, it's easy to fall into violent, unhealthy, or imbalanced sexual partnerships. The dom-sub relationship is one of them, but sexual wounds in general are bound to come up on your journey. You're a naturally sensual, sexual, and seductive person, even if you aren't aware of it. Being so magnetic, feminine, and ultra sensitive, moreover emotionally deep makes you quite seductive. Merged with your innocence, you tend to fall for people who want to use or take advantage of you, or in worst case scenarios, abuse you.

Carl Jung's *universal archetypes* can help you to understand and integrate your sexuality fully, in a way that is healthy, balanced, and loving to yourself. Unconscious wounds, triggers, and traumas can often manifest in sexual partnerships. Therefore, shadow work is essential. This is the dark, repressed, and hidden aspects of you. We have an individual shadow and a collective shadow, but there is also the empath shadow. Accepting, embracing, and balancing your shadow traits can help you to find the light, working towards enlightenment through finding harmony and embodiment.

Traumas and Ancestral Wounds

Your traumas and ancestral wounds are issues that have grown with you since childhood, core root blockages and distortions that come with the human experience. They are the subconscious and repressed parts of you, and they run deep, being part of your individual and the collective psyche. As an empath, you take on everyone's pain, suffering, and internal battles. You feel everything so deeply that you experience them as if they're you. This means that even when you're not in a dark or introspective space yourself, and you're in a process of healing, you still seem to receive and absorb everyone else's "stuff." This only adds to the trauma more. You absorb people's personal traumas, fears, and deep wounds while trying to heal or make sense of your own. This certainly happens before you reach adulthood and spiritual maturity. Due to such heightened sensitivities, you can become lost to multiple realities that you may think are good for you, such as playing everyone's free therapist, healer, or caregiver, but actually drain you. Not only do they drain you, they deplete you of your energy, time, love, resources, and ability to hold space in a way that allows you to also receive, such as in a professional setting. I can honestly share that I played everybody's "free therapist" until my mid to late twenties, and I was homeless, heartbroken, and completely lost at many stages of my life. Empath trauma runs deep. All humans experience trauma, as all of us are capable of empathy. Yet empaths feel so deeply it's like you actually become that person, plant, or animal. With such heightened psychic sensitivities, you merge with another's entire frequency, aura, and identity; you feel their feelings, take on their emotions, and bond with their trauma or pain.

Without even being aware, you naturally tune in to invisible and behind-the-scenes pains, traumas and wounds, and bring them to light. This is incredibly powerful and can be used for great benefit; if used correctly, with love, compassion, and kindness, you can become a real gem in someone's life. If used negatively, however, i.e. unconsciously and without boundaries or consent (asking for someone's permission to give advice or tune into their aura), this can be dangerous. Firstly, you can royally piss people off, not everyone wants your healing. Secondly, it's a violation of sorts, potentially an abuse of your power. Your intentions will always be pure, and this is why there is no negative karma attached to empaths and their abilities. You possess superpowers for real, and your intentions will always be rooted in serving with love, helping others, and using your gifts for good and moral cause. Nevertheless, you can't project your own pain and insecurities or unresolved trauma on others. Whilst you're doing it, you wouldn't ever assume that this is the reality of what's occurring. "What, projecting my pain?" You may be wondering... Yes, dear empath. Trying to heal every human you come across is a projection of pain and unhealed trauma. You're not a martyr, nor are you supposed to treat informal, social, or random meetings as professional therapy, healing, or counseling sessions.

So, not only do you have your own trauma and wounds to work through, but you will also likely be under the illusion that it's your responsibility to take on everyone else's suffering. This, 1. Slows down your healing journey, 2. Makes you codependency, lost, and confused, and 3. Perpetuates toxic and illusory cycles and chapters. Your key to enlightenment and personal awakening is to take "me time"- soul search. Explore yourself, rest, and go within. Become the Hermit or Lone Wolf, but consciously. Work with divinatory and healing systems and tools like the Tarot, crystals, Reiki, sound therapy, meditation, and astrology or numerology. Through self-healing, divination, and commitment to self-love, you can become the change you wish to see. On this note, be careful of something known as ***spiritual bypassing***. Spiritual bypassing is something many sensitive and instinctive people do, implying you only choose to see the positive. This prevents true growth and healing. You miss out on, deny, or dismiss multiple other avenues and doorways to healing and self-knowledge. Spiritual bypassing also signifies only choosing to see or feel good emotions. Sadness, pain, anger, despair, grief, and the need to scream, shout, or express your truest feelings are denied.

I alongside many empaths I have known on my path can confirm that anger is something we homo lumens choose to deny and reject. We think it makes us "less" human, "less" spiritual, and "less" worthy of all good things. Empaths are generally quite good with sadness and grief, but *anger* coupled with hostility, aggression, and the need to show our worth, talent, or capacity for love and attention can be very hard for us to accept. It's the primal and animalistic part of ourselves, and empaths tend to be more of the light, in the spiritual body. Quite simply, many empaths believe primal emotions make us less human, and must be overlooked or repressed. This only perpetuates the cycle of trauma and blocks healing from ancestral and karmic wounds on many deep levels.

Let's look at the ways trauma can manifest itself in your life:

- Spending a lot of time alone, to an unhealthy, self-sabotaging, and self-destructive extent.
- Escapism and getting lost in fantasy; creating a dream world and escaping from reality.
- Addictions including food, alcohol, tobacco, substance, drug, television, porn, and gaming addictions.
- Self-consciousness, inability to speak your truth, and blocks to self-expression, sharing your talents, and being more bold and courageous.
- Repressing, denying, and dismissing or escaping from pain; blocking out real suffering, grief, and heartache.
- Believing some emotions are inferior and therefore in need of complete dismissal (anger, a need to explode from time to time- showing your pain to the world).
- Going within to the point of extreme introversion, isolation, and lone wolf syndrome.
- Not being able to connect, experience intimacy, platonic and/or romantic, or have lasting and meaningful relationships.
- Fears of public places, social gatherings, and crowds, or even conversations that involve more than 3- 5 people.
- Oversensitive in intimate relationships, hyperemotional, and cut off from family, love, romance, sexual intimacy, community, or society.

- Attracting narcissists, energy vampires, and oppressive personalities... You can be a sh*t magnet!

Romance and Sexuality: Soulmates and Transcending Karmic Cycles

An amazingly interesting topic linked to your ultimate destiny, to become *homo lumens*, or close to, is the innate gravitational pull you have towards "higher soulmate love." This means leaving behind toxic and karmic cycles, chapters, and preferences in love. Actually, without meaning to instill fear, this is quite essential when observing your submissive nature, moreover the tendency you have towards attracting abusive types. Empaths are romantic, sweet, and nurturing. We live for love, least to mention a fantastical type of "fairytale love." Negatively this can give into toxic belief systems and behaviors, yet, positively, we understand there is a higher law. There is a higher power. We have karmic soulmates and higher love soulmates. This is something all empaths understand on some instinctive and subtle level, and something many of us go on to explore further in depth. This is quite a big topic, so let's break this down.

Romance, Sweetness, and Harmony: Empath Essentials In Love

Romance, sweetness, and harmony are empath essentials, staples in love and life. You are a lover, you live for love, harmony, sensitivity, nurturing, kindness, and unconditional surrender to someone who only has your best interests at heart. You are someone with a slightly whimsical and spacey aura, you can be away with the fairies. Positively, this makes you a beautiful lover for someone who doesn't mind your submissive and sweet nature. You're not cold, calculated, analytical, dominant, or controlling in love. You can lack charm, charisma, and confidence, qualities shared by fire and air signs. But you are pure, honest, and sincere, moreover incredibly loyal once in love. Empaths crave loyalty and security, despite giving off a bit of a lone wolf, nomadic, or free spirited vibe. These projected images couldn't be any further from reality- empaths project these persona into the ether to protect themselves. You have a fragile heart, so any projected image of a "fierce and independent lone wolf" or "free spirited earth wanderer" in love is just to protect your heart. You're sensitive deep, and fall in love quite easily when you give your heart, you give all of you. You can be codependent, but the positive manifestation of this is that you trust and surrender into sacred union. When the vibe is right, compatibility and divine flow is present, and harmony, mutual understanding, and genuine emotions are there, your yielding nature opens portals to higher love.

Interesting fact: The sign of the empath is Pisces, and Venus is exalted (*in its best position*) in Pisces. Venus is the planet of love, romance, beauty, sensuality, pleasure, and female sexuality... this is an additional piece of wisdom to store in your memory bank.

Fairytale Love: A Curse or A Blessing?

Fairytale love is something very common among empaths, and has its successes and downfalls. Starting with the negative, idealized notions of fairytale love leads to narcissistic abuse, relationships with cold and domineering characters who do not have your best interests at heart. Your strong sense of idealism can lead to many illusory and fantasy-based notions, such as that a real-life prince or knight in shining armor will rescue you. Sorry to say, Repunzel was a Disney character, and Disney is here to provide us with some valuable life lessons. Living in reality can be difficult for you. I myself was in love with a childhood best friend until my late twenties-early thirties, so I have compassion for you. We mistake platonic intimacy, connection, friendship, mutual feelings of respect and kindness, and brief moments of romance or chemistry for them being "the one." We see everything through emotional, instinctive, and intuitive lenses- we lack rationality and logic entirely. This signifies that we make mistakes, succumb to fantasies, and live in a state of illusion and confusion. Just as we are misunderstood by the world, we misinterpret the world, at times.

Your idealized notions of fairytale love can leave you stuck on a soulmate for years to a decade +. It's not healthy, moreover it's extremely self-harming. Cycles of trauma, hardship, and destruction ensure when you fail to accept this folly of yours. (Trust me, I've been there.) Fairytale love is usually rooted in the faulty and distorted belief system that everyone is on your wavelength. It almost always occurs before you realize that narcissistic characters and narcissistic abuse are real, they exist, and you are the perfect target for their gaslighting and manipulations. Narcissists feed off of empaths, quite literally. They drain your light, life force, and self-esteem. They use you as an energy source in the same way Neo was plugged in, unconscious and unaware, in the Matrix. Before you awaken to certain truths combined with your own powers and abilities, you are a fuel source. This ultimately affects your romantic and sexual relationships, in addition to your capacity to attract grounded, balanced, and real love. Fortunately, it's just a cycle. Most empaths transcend the fairytale love stage.

Prone to Extreme Submissiveness and Codependency

Extreme submissiveness and codependency has already been covered through these chapters, but it is something that's worthy of its own heading. Reflect on all of the information presented thus far. Do you feel you're in a codependent cycle, or are there ways you can heal? What reflections have you written in your journals or dream diary, and how can they help you now?! Do you feel balanced, a bit more playful and cerebral or intellectual than your previous extremely submissive self, or are you still processing trauma and pain? Extreme submission, without boundaries, is a direct result of unhealed and unprocessed trauma, or, at the least, heartbreak.

An Amazing Lover, Giver, and Nurturing Family Wo/man

Empaths are extraordinary lovers, givers, and nurturing family people. In addition to all the creative, artistic, and healing gifts, empaths can be quite domestic. We enjoy taking care of people, and this trickles into home and family life. Once grounded and balanced- older, wiser, and maturer (less naive and self-sacrificing!), we make loving caregivers at home. This means enjoying cooking, gardening, and introducing beautiful creativity and imagination in a practical or domestic situation. Environments benefit from the empath touch, which can include feng shui, beautifully designed living arrangements, or putting a midas touch on any living area. We love to cook, clean, and please our lovers, as long as we feel we're genuinely being of service in some way. We ask ourselves, 'will this enhance our relationship?' 'Will my domestic or practical gifts expand love and connection?' 'How can I be of service at home to be the best lover, friend, and partner?' We're givers with massive hearts, and we live to pleasure and please. You may be wanting to stop and think, isn't everyone like this? No, actually. Some people are selfish, takers, and cold. Some people are mean-spirited, lack empathy, or are inconsiderate and self-centered. Not everyone is like an empath. This is why you should aim for someone compatible, someone who sees your empath soul. This may rock some boats, but I am sorry to say, astrology does play an integral role in the empath nature. For example, if someone has no strong earth or water placement (earth and water are yin or feminine in nature), they are highly unlikely to be an empath. An individual needs *at least one* earth or water Sun, Moon, or Rising placement to be considered an empath. *There is a Disclaimer on page 128 to add some more depth to this.*

A Natural Duty to Escape Karmic Cycles

You find throughout life that you're pulled towards higher things, and this makes you want to escape karmic cycles. For instance, friendship groups and circles that once brought you a lot of joy, fun, or learning and self-growth no longer appeal to you once you start to awaken to cosmic and spiritual laws. Lvers, friends, and acquaintances associated with youth become boring, toxic, or totally unappealing. You start to feel that they limit your growth, keep you blocked and stagnant, and misalign you with your true path. You witness how you miss opportunities the more you stay connected to such people, places, and timelines. It's sad, you will cry, and you will feel guilty, as this is your nature. However, breaking free from such chains is necessary for your evolution, more importantly, your service to others and the world. In love and business or profession/vocation, karmic cycles are not a "forever" solution. They provide valuable lessons, pearls of wisdom, and gems of insight, yet your destiny lies in something greater. Purely in love, karmic cycles from childhood and youth are usually linked to at least one sexual relationship, potentially more.

You can see the karmic journey in your kundalini, or your Rainbow body. Energy begins at the Root and makes its way up to the Crown. We repeat certain stories and timeliness, as well as frequencies, patterns of behavior, and life chapters, until we realize that they no longer serve us (karmic/toxic stories)... or are in best interest with our higher selves (transcended/ascended and higher law/love realities). Linked to this is your blood family; some empaths choose to cut family members out temporarily to heal and find themselves. There's too much trauma, faulty beliefs, and hostility or blocks present in family bonds. I would suggest this shouldn't be forever, putting blocks on family should only be *temporary*, until your Crown is fully active and your whole Rainbow Body balanced and awakened. Other experts might tell you differently, but I would suggest this is an idealized notion, and that they're further neglecting logic and balanced perspectives!

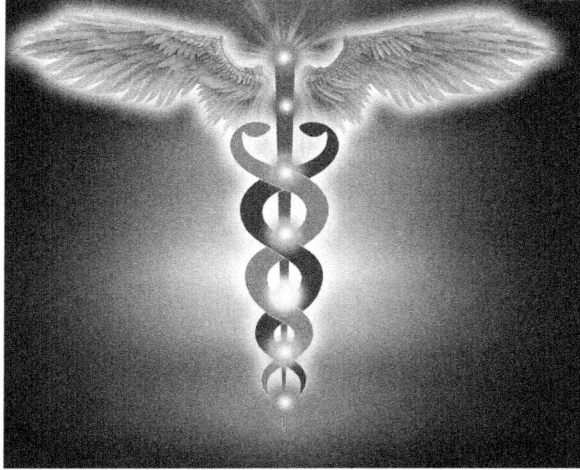

Aligned to Higher Love… Soulmates… Twin Flame Ideals

Finally, you are very open to higher ideals, belief systems, and possibilities, including higher love soulmates or the concept of twin flames. Higher love soulmates are those you've shared a journey with, individually and together. You've risen from the lows of karmic love, the toxic and limiting cycles that keep you bound. You've chosen a higher path, so a higher love soulmate is someone compatible- your Rainbow Bodies match. You've both undergone a long and a deep process of healing, releasing trauma and old wounds, and self-mastery. You practice what you preach, you've walked the talk! You haven't just got stuck in the philosopher stage, but actually made the changes; to heal, rise above family and ancestral wounds, and become the best possible person you can be. Your chakras are alive and awakened, as well as balanced, harmonized, and activated. Divine love is certainly present. Higher soulmate love can be initiated in youth or later in life depending on your unique soul's blueprint, the challenges and choices you set to make (before incarnation), and a combination of fate and free will.

Twin flames share the same qualities as higher love soulmates, but go a stage further. This is a true life partner and power coupled material. A twin flame is your soul's perfect mirror, you are two bodies sharing one soul. You've known each other for countless lifetimes, have possibly been married in a past life, or have chosen to journey together as different soulmates (a human-pet relationship, mother-son/daughter, best friends, etc.) to understand each other's souls on a deeper level. In this life, you come together in holy matrimony, in sacred union. Twin flames always have some higher spiritual or conscious mission, for example creating art or music that will inspire the world, or both being healers, inventors, or humanitarians. Your twin flame is your soul's counterpart, a divine reflection, and your ideal lover, life partner, and mirror. Not all empaths choose a twin flame, and many would say this is an idealized "fairytale" type love. This is partly true. From a logical and rational perspective, I guess it is. But we empaths aren't logical or analytical, are we... As emotional and intuitive creatures who, unlike most humans, are capable of unconditional love coupled with agape love- selfless, universal, love; I would suggest the concept of twin flame soul union is very real.

You can see some articles I wrote explaining this topic of exploration, in depth, here. Make up your own mind! Soul search, dive deep, and be authentic with your desires, needs, and emotions. First and foremost, always choose the way of the heart. ✧

- 7 Karmic Relationship Stages Explained (1[2])
- Soulmate Vs Twin Flame Vs Karmic: Key Differences (2[3])
- 1111 Angel Number TWIN FLAME (3[4])

---

[2]
https://ncrw.org/karmic-relationship-stages/?fbclid=IwAR0p3SGrmm8Te0991vG3X2qthaYWmVHl4DMLbYztH8xROfv5vjdYc6BWg_g

[3]
https://ncrw.org/soulmate-vs-twin-flame-vs-karmic/?fbclid=IwAR1GCS7TXxDZnC9MJXkfZDf2EX7bktvAQ7eOsaSLtV23B1BHfzQdEiNmFE0

[4] https://ncrw.org/1111-angel-number-twin-flame/

Why Empaths are the Next Stage in the Evolutionary Cycle

Fortunately, you can overcome your pain and trauma and evolve into the magnificent beings you incarnated here to be. Empaths are arguably the next stage in the evolutionary cycle. Your destiny is to embody unconditional love, advanced empathy, and universal compassion (with boundaries). Before you can fully step into any one of your chosen or given roles, it is essential that you practice unconditional love for yourself, not just for everyone else. Loving you and treating yourself with the respect, kindness, and care you deserve allows you to be the beautiful empathic being you were born to be. wish to fully be. Low self-esteem, taking oneself too seriously, and sacrificing your own joys and peace for others- not knowing how to "lighten up" or experience fun and play won't do, in the long-run. Only when your cup is full can you manifest your intentions for healing and being of service. It all starts with self-love and acceptance.

As A Child...

As an empathic child, you were almost certainly told to stop being so sensitive, shy, and withdrawn. You were shamed, scolded by your parents, assuming you had "normal" parents (not mega spiritual or empathic ones), and were made fun of at school. You were likely the lone wolf, oddball, and black sheep, and didn't know how to ground or stabilize your feelings and insights. You were wise beyond years, yet deeply misunderstood. You were bullied, victimized, and told to stop being so sensitive, which limited your powers. Not only did this misdirection limit you, but it suppressed you, further turning off essential innate knowledge and healing avenues. Your light was dimmed, possibly put out altogether, and you were labeled as weird, strange, or a loner. Empath children need to keep to themselves, to recharge, and to gather their strength. You need a lot of time to recharge, rejuvenate, and replenish your energies. And, you are often left out, cut out of social groups and activities, and left to deal with tricky emotions and belief systems by your parents and teachers. You saw from an advanced and elevated frequency, but others did not, so you were forced to become very introspective, withdrawn, and isolated to make sense of your impressions and the world around you.

---

1. Empaths are Earth Angels

Empaths are the Earth Angels of the world, the highly evolved beings incarnated to help change your humanity's vibration and raise humanity's consciousness. You're wise beyond years, deeply perceptive, and concerned with the wellbeing of mankind, the animals of the world, and the planet. As an Earth Angel, you are in tune with multiple planes and exist in multiple realms and avatars. This allows you to both hold space and engage in personal and planetary healing, contributing to the global shift and ascension. You're genuine, sincere, and heal a lot of people with your loving thoughts and capacity to shine light wherever you go. You embody the spirit of a healer and dreamer while knowing you need to retain your personal boundaries, to stay grounded and centered. This is how you can make real change in the world.

2. Empaths are Saintlike

Although you have some self-sacrificing tendencies to overcome, you are saintlike with the capacity for real ascended master status. Your energy ripples out into space, affecting virtually everyone you come across. Even the bad characters your intuition tells you to put strong boundaries up against or even block out of your energy field, you help. Your energy speaks for itself. You carry yourself well with grace and class, many people think empaths are super-spacey or away with the fairies, moreover lost in fantasy land. But when healed and evolved, empaths are incredibly grounded. You apply a practical spirituality to daily life, which includes all of your beliefs, thoughts, morals, conversations, and attitudes to life, self, and being. Like Mother Teresa or some of the world's most loved and well-known archangels and angels, you know how to embody unconditional love coupled with universal compassion.

3. Empaths are Selfless

Empaths are selfless, live with heart, and are full of soul. Living with heart may sound like something all humans do, and although it shocks your sweet heart, the reality is this is not the case. Not all humans are heart-centered individuals. Not everyone is capable of empathy, humility, or grace. Everyone isn't noble like you, or attuned to the higher mind and Higher Self. Some people really are cold, rude, self-centered, egotistical, and all about the 'I.' Some people like to use people, or get a kick out of other people's suffering. There are some selfish and heartless, i.e. not living with heart, people on this earth. Empaths choose a higher timeline, an earth reality that allows them to live in tune with the divine...

4. Empaths are in tune with the Divine

Empaths are in tune with the divine, a higher and ethereal reality where spiritual life force and concepts shine through in every moment. You live in tune with Mother Earth, ancestral forces, as well as celestial heavenly ones. Your feet bind with the earth in a way that enables you to perpetually heal and rejuvenate- empaths have active feet chakras.

You're also Crown chakra awake and activate, your Crown being a direct link to the infinite, cosmic consciousness, and higher perspective realities and timelines. Faith, clairvoyance, inspiration, a link to the Unknown, mysticism, spiritual healing powers, and everything to do with higher, spiritual, and angelic frequencies and abilities are connected to your Crown. Divine inspiration combined with universal archetypes flow to you. You're an amazing friend, lover, partner, family or community member, and soul brother or sister, and to many. Empaths tend to be gems to a lot of people, as well as a kindred spirit and respected member of your communities. This is because you birth divine insights and revelations that can inspire a lot of people. You live as a channel, and this allows you to shine light, wisdom, and truth into the collective.

5. Empaths are capable of Unconditional Love and Universal Compassion

As a natural telepath, animal whisperer/communicator, healer, counselor, caregiver, visionary, dreamer, psychic, and seer or spiritual guide, you embody advanced levels of unconditional love. Empaths truly are homo lumens, are new species of humans. Like snakes who sense vibrations through the ether, bats who use echolocation (a unique superpower) to see sound, and dolphins who communicate through supersonic waves, telepathically, you are capable of many advanced gifts. The secret is an active kundalini, which occurs when all of your chakras are awake and balanced or harmonized. This manifests through the copious amounts of spiritual healing, self-development, and self-care work you do. When you do the inner work, you become whole, integrated, and enlightened; enlightenment is simply becoming and finding the light.

6. Empaths are connected to the Superconsciousness

From astral insights to advanced lucid, dreaming, and waking life experiences and abilities, empaths are clearly in tune with mystical and spiritual forces. All humans are capable of this, but we empaths are much more in tune, in an organic and natural way. Things come naturally to us. We are able to do, see, and attain things that many people need a lot of help accessing. We've incarnated here with memories from past lives, our soul's plan available in full force, and a direct cord to our Akashic Records, the angelic and ascended master realms, and lots of hidden portals and chords to ancient and divine knowledge, self-awareness, and creative and spiritual mastery. The purpose? To live out our intended plan, to help, heal, and serve. An empath without a mission is like a bird without wings; we require purpose, passion, and a clear vision of our path to manifest, create, and achieve.

Empaths are the next stage in the evolutionary cycle because we actively shape, create, and restructure life, reality, through our thoughts, actions,

and intentions. We are powerful creators and manifestors, moreover lovers. We don't hate or fight, we don't give into the temptations of society with all of its distorted beliefs, conditioning, and false directions. Our DNA awakens, ignites, and initiates for collective and personal healing...
Through unlocking spiritual gifts, spirit itself becomes more accessible, and because we are all connected, more people awaken to their own inner gifts. An empath's individual journey is intrinsically connected to the collective journey, and this is why it is essential for all empaths to wake up, embrace their empathic destiny, and realize that sensitivity is a superpower and blessings, not a curse!

Chapter 4: Chakra and Color Healing

Looking at the Chakra System: Harmonizing, Balancing, & Integrating

All of those childhood traumas, unconscious wounds, and patterns of behavior no longer play a part in your life. You are now free to shine your superpowers out to the world; it begins with unconditional love, acceptance, and empathy for yourself. One of the most powerful tools for an empath, in addition to astrology and divinatory systems like tarot and crystals, is chakra and color therapy. These are two "empath essentials."

Your chakras are powerful portals that connect to physical organs and body parts. Chakra translates as energy portal or energy wheel in ancient Sanskrit, one of the most advanced languages and cultures. You have 7 main chakras beginning at your Root or pelvis and ending at your Crown or the top of your head. You also have your feet and palm chakras, the feet connecting you to Mother Earth and her ancestral healing energies, and the hands or palm chakras enabling you to channel healing energy for self and others. You then have your Earth Star and Soul Star chakras, two less known energy portals, but very real. These are located below your feet and above your crown, and link to the most powerful ancestral/earthy and higher/celestial energies. There is finally the Thymus chakra, in between your Heart and Throat, symbolizing karmic energy, love, empathy, compassion, forgiveness, self-respect, and integration. The Thymus chakra activates when you've come to terms with karmic cycles, higher laws and perspectives, and cosmic themes. It's usually awakened in people who have healed their karma, transcended toxic cycles, and made peace with their past, present, and future lives, and all of the challenges that accompany. It is considered the "seat of the soul" to some, although I would personally call it a bridge linking your lower and higher self, which further activates once you've embarked on a journey of karma and wound healing.

So, to explore yourself further and heal on multiple and profound levels, you must become familiar with your chakras. Here is an essential guide to chakra healing:

- All illness, diseases, and imbalances originate on some subtle frequency. Technically speaking, all diseases, also known as "dis-ease," some aspect of yourself being disconnected and at discomfort with itself, begins in the soul planes. This then trickles down into the spiritual, astral, ethereal, mental, and emotional bodies, before then becoming manifest in the physical. Remember that the ethereal body is an extension of the physical.

- Any block, ailment, or imbalance begins in some mental, emotional, spiritual, or core wounded distortion. For example, you can't seem to attract prosperity or live in abundance, this implies you're stuck in "poverty consciousness." (Poverty is a mindset.) You can't seem to find true love, you're still holding onto wounds and trauma or pain surrounding past love and heartache. You frequently experience tricky emotions or emotional chaos and disparity, you haven't yet healed your wounds or done the inner work needed... The list goes on.
- Every sound heard, sight witnessed, and touch experienced contributes to the holistic Self. All of your beliefs, conditioned thought patterns, inner emotional responses, spiritual understandings, and innate psychological perspectives and reasoning have their origins in something internal. We are shaped by our experiences, observations, hardships, struggles, interactions, the sensory stimuli in our physical environments, and inner biological factors. We're governed by both subconscious and conscious forces.
- Your chakras, when healed and unblocked, help to bring subconscious forces and blocks to light. They symbolize everything internal that needs to be smoothed out, harmonized, and brought into balance and equilibrium. When your chakras are unblocked, this leads to a kundalini awakening, your kundalini being symbolic of psychic instincts, spiritual powers, sensuality, life force, creativity, libido- sexual health, and longevity.

Let's now look at the chakra system to expand your awareness of how the beautiful gift of empathy can be harnessed through deeper inner work, for self-mastery.

The Root Chakra

The Root chakra is your foundation, your sense of security, grounding, and survival. It relates to self-preservation, connection to the earth and your own body, physical vitality, libido, sexual energy, and life force. The Root chakra sparks kundalini energy that leads to wholeness, healing, and harmony on all levels, between your subtle energy bodies. Your kundalini is your serpent power, the snake-like coil of energy that flows from your base up your spine to your head or Crown chakra. Physically, it is responsible for your vitality, physical health and energy levels, and sexual energy. It also corresponds to your physical chi and life-force energy, and on the mental and emotional planes links to mental power, emotional wisdom and maturity, and psychic and intuitive abilities. The associated colors are red (primary) and brown and black. The element is earth.

If the root chakra is blocked, then all the other chakras will be blocked. As an empath, you can often be in your head and out of your body, so problems can arise; disconnection from your body, others, and society, impracticalities, issues in finances and the ability to make or save money, and blocks to intimacy. You forget to think, analyze, and be rational, always choosing feelings and instincts. You tend to sense things rather than think intellectually, also succumbing to self-sacrifice. A healthy sense of self links to the Root chakra, without a healthy ego, you run the risk of falling prey to predatory characters. I.e. ones who are focused on survival, security, and self-preservation. Everything begins at the Root, and as an empath this signifies coming to terms with your physical existence. You're not just about emotional intelligence, sensitivity, and wisdom or spiritual gifts and powers; you are a spiritual being having a physical experience, and this means embracing all practical, material, and physical aspects of life. To access higher spiritual gifts, your Root must be unblocked, so this chakra is essential for working with.

Ways to work with your Root chakra

1. Crystal therapy: Obsidian, Black Tourmaline, Smoky Quartz, Jet, Garnet, Red Jasper, Hematite, Bloodstone, and Black Onyx
2. Daily mantra keyword focus: Security, survival, self-preservation, vitality, physical instincts, libido, protection, longevity, and grounding
3. Herbs, plants, and essential oils: Ginger, Turmeric, Ashwagandha, Dandelion, Clove, and Raspberry Leaf... Essential oils: Frankincense, Myrth, and Cedarwood

The Sacral Chakra

The Sacral chakra is also known as your emotion, creativity, and sex center. It symbolizes friendliness, warmth, emotional intelligence, vulnerability, and sensitivity, romance, intimacy, creativity, artistic talents, sociability, sexual desires and fantasies, the imagination, and subconscious forces. Emotions, creativity, and sexuality are known to be linked. In other words, blocks in one of these will lead to blocks in the others, while smooth energy flow results in positive vibrations to the others. The Sacral is one of the areas where the empaths have the most problems. Many repressed emotions, traumas and wounds become stored over time, in the Sacral. As you will see in the next chakra, this strongly affects the Solar Plexus, your sense of vitality, ambition, willpower, self-empowerment, and confidence. Blocks in your Sacral prevent intimacy, companionship, and authentic and deep bonding, things essential for your empathic nature. Sexual fears and wounds come into the Sacral, as do creative and artistic blocks. This inevitably stops visionary and imaginative flow. As for emotions, all aspects of emotional relating and bonding, including emotional intelligence, empathy, and sensitivity are part of the Sacral chakra's domain. Interpersonal relationships of all kinds can be healed and soothed with the Sacral, as well as finding a greater sense of fun, joy, vitality, self-expression, and playfulness. The related color is orange and the element is water.

Ways to work with your Sacral chakra

1. Crystal therapy: Carnelian, Moonstone, Orange Calcite, Pearl, Orange Aventurine, Sardonyx, Sunstone, and Tiger's Eye
2. Daily mantra keyword focus: Emotions, intuition, feelings, sensitivity, romance, self-love, creativity, imagination, artistic gifts, sociability, relationships, and sexuality
3. Herbs, plants, and essential oils: Hibiscus, Cinnamon, Chamomile, Damiana, Raspberry Leaf, and Cloves... Essential oils: Ylang Ylang, Orange, Patchouli, Clary Sage, Chamomile, and Neroli

The Solar Plexus Chakra

The Solar Plexus chakras relates to your sense of self-empowerment, self-esteem, ambition, willpower, and confidence. It is your ability to act on your goals, be high-flying and high-achieving, and follow through on your purpose. Purpose, passion, and personal power and authority are what can be unblocked and gained with Solar Plexus. Confidence, self-worth, and self-esteem issues come into this chakra. It's your place of will, empowerment, and vitality, moreover how ambitious, determined, and tenacious you are... To plan, achieve, dream big, create long-term goals, and so forth. Intellectual power arises from the Solar Plexus, as does creative, spiritual, and sexual energy. All of the qualities from the Root and Sacral must come up through the Solar Plexus, to reach the Heart and higher chakras. Blocks here can mess your entire chakra system up, which includes your subtle bodies. You can work with the Solar Plexus to become more sunny, positive, courageous, bold, expressive, passionate, self-authoritative, and optimistic. This chakra has a great effect on mood swings, low moods, and a lack of masculine strength, life force, and personal power. You can increase integrity, nobility, and idealistic elements to your personality when working with the Solar Plexus in synergy with the Third Eye or Crown. Emotional balance and harmony are said to flow here, specifically in its connection with the Sacral. As an empath, it's important to energize your Solar Plexus regularly for self-protection, self-alignment, and commitment to your life path, purpose, and destiny or legacy. The color for this chakra is yellow, sometimes golden-yellow, and the element is fire.

Ways to work with your Solar Plexus chakra

1. Crystal therapy: Citrine, Amber, Tiger's Eye, Yellow Jasper, Yellow Topaz, Lemon Quartz, Sunstone, and Pyrite
2. Daily mantra keyword focus: Ambition, self-esteem, personal authority, courage, confidence, self-empowerment, positivity, optimism, expression, purpose, alignment, and youthfulness
3. Herbs, plants, and essential oils: Peppermint, Cayenne, Lemongrass, Goldenrod, Essential oils: Geranium, Ginger, Grapefruit, Black Pepper, Lemon, Lemongrass, and Sandalwood

Heart Chakra

Your Heart chakra is your central chakra connecting the lower self and higher self. It is the bridge or cord between the two, and its health and harmony is essential to bringing out your best abilities and qualities. Symbolism and characteristics of the Heart include: empathy, tolerance, kindness, patience, compassion, unconditional love, self-love, non-jugement, generosity, humility, modesty, respect for self and others, a connection to Mother Earth and the natural world, and natural charm and charisma. Emotional wisdom flows up through the lower chakras to the Heart, which is then transformed into visionary, intuitive, and intellectual power and inspiration in the higher centers. The Heart can be worked with for all matters of relationships, self-expression, and self-development . Empath healing closely links to the Heart, as well as finding a soulmate or partner on your wavelength. A strong Heart chakra allows you to be centered, balanced, and aligned to your true path, in addition to attracting the right people on your journey. Blocks to self-love and romantic intimacy can be overcome, and life force energy flows abundantly to your Throat, Third Eye, and Crown. All empaths have a strong Heart chakra. The associated color is green and the elements are earth and ether/spirit.

Ways to work with your Heart chakra

1. Crystal therapy: Rose Quartz, Rhodochrosite, Green Aventurine, Amazonite, Malachite, Jade, Chrysoprase, Kunzite, Moldavite, Moss Agate, Jade, and Peridot
2. Daily mantra keyword focus: Empathy, self-love, universal compassion, tolerance, kindness, generosity, sensitivity, patience, emotional balance and harmony, nobility, and integrity

3. Herbs, plants, and essential oils: Rose, Neem, Moringa, Rosemary, Hawthorn Leaf, Motherwort, Lemon Balm, Vervain, and Lavender... Essential oils: Jasmine, Lavender, Rose, Geranium Ylang Ylang, and Bergamot

Throat Chakra

The Throat chakra is your center for communication, self-expression, and inspiration linking to the spiritual, angelic, and ethereal planes. Multidimensional communication and astral gifts associated with the empath nature come into this chakra. Also, direct and assertive communication, charm, charisma, sociability, personal confidence to speak your truth and share your wisdom and talents... These can all be developed. The ability to communicate is essential in all empath professions, vocations, and modes of service. You can lack direct, bold, and assertive communication, and this is a real problem area in life. You can also be shy, timid, and overly reserved or humble and modest. Working with your Throat chakra will release tension and blocks to self-expression on multiple planes and dimensions. From business partnerships to creative bonds and family and friendship connections, in addition to self-talk and storytelling, the capacity you have to be an amazing poet, speaker, or teacher, or counselor and so forth; the Throat chakra is your key to personal awakening. Personal and collective truth also comes into the Throat chakra. Angelic contact and communication can be fine-tuned, and imaginative, artistic, and soulful gifts can be amplified. The Throat relates to all aspects of wisdom and truth sharing, talent and gift expression, and opening up about your feelings, deepest desires, and emotions. Vulnerability and transparency can be found and increased. The associated color is blue and the element is air.

Ways to work with your Throat chakra

1. Crystal therapy: Lapis Lazuli, Amazonite, Aquamarine, Blue Kyanite, Blue Lace Agate, Turquoise, Sapphire, Azurite, Chrysocolla, Blue Chalcedony, and Angelite
2. Daily mantra keyword focus: Self-expression, communication, inspiration, angelic contact, truth, integrity, nobility, individuality, intention, imagination, and creative inspiration
3. Herbs, plants, and essential oils: Fennel, Black Pepper, Slippery Elm, Sage, Thyme, Chamomile, Calendula, and Marshmallow... Essential oils: Basil, Chamomile, Cypress, Eucalyptus, Clary Sage, Sage, Spearmint, Peppermint, Bergamot, and Pine

Third Eye Chakra

Your Third Eye is your seat of consciousness, your higher wisdom, sight, and visionary center. It brings the qualities of vision, idealism, cognitive and cerebral power, intellect, wit, intelligence, intuition, extrasensory perception, and psychic gifts. Psychic, intuitive, and spiritual gifts flow here. As an empath, you grow up with a strong Third Eye chakra, at least in comparison to most people in society. Your'e not normal, nor do you strive to be; even as a child, you saw things people didn't. You possess a unique sense of high morals and ethics, spiritual visions and ideologies, and belief systems that are contrary to the norm. You will have experienced strong bouts of compassion, empathy, and love for animals, planet earth, and other humans, although the world, society, your teachers, etc. would have told you that you were living in fantasy land. You were seen as a dreamer with idealistic standards, yet, to you, your beliefs and opinions formed were perfectly natural. A key example is this: I remember one profound memory from secondary school where we were discussing whaling as a sport, killing beautifully sentient whales and the reasons some humans gave for doing so. As predicted, many people saw it as something normal or even justifiable, many people gave rational and logical justifications. During the class debate, I remember sitting there wanting to cry, thinking 'what is wrong with these people.... I must be from a different planet?' These were my genuine feelings.

I felt an energy shift, I felt like I was floating in some timeless holographic chamber. I felt completely out of place in that classroom, with these young people and my teacher justifying whale killing. It was insane to me. My gut instincts and intuition told me there was no rational, emotional, spiritual or otherwise explanation for this insanity. That was my empath self talking. Using my psychic gifts now, traveling back to that scene, I would be able to suggest that there were around 3- 4 other empaths in the room, based on the deep shift in energy and spiritual awareness I felt. They were also quiet! (I did actually share my rather "out there" perspective, of which case it was dismissed and if I remember correctly even ridiculed by my teacher.)

Going back to Third Eye chakra symbolism, we empaths see, perceive, and feel from multidimensional and even cosmic perspectives. Our sight and intellect is rooted in compassion, universal love, and higher spiritual ideals and values. We believe in the unity of all things, interconnectedness and oneness too. We see all as one big global family, plants, nature, and animals included. We are open to spiritual phenomena, psychic gifts, and advanced lucid and dream states. Lucid dreaming, astral travel, and receiving subconscious and Higher Self guidance and wisdom in dreams are linked to the Third Eye chakra. This energy center acts as a merging of subconscious and conscious wisdom and knowledge. It's the seat of the psyche, soul, and primary empath personality. It's also core to a number of holistic, extrasensory, and intuitive powers, in addition to telepathy, clairvoyance, clairaudience, and clairsentience. Wisdom, higher truth, and evolved wisdom are part of the Third Eye chakra's domain. The corresponding colors are purple and indigo, and the related element is ether/spirit.

Ways to work with your Third Eye chakra

1. Crystal therapy: Amethyst, Sodalite, Ametrine, Celestite, Lapis Lazuli, Sugilite, Labradorite, Moonstone, Fluorite, and Lepidolite
2. Daily mantra keyword focus: Vision, prophecy, clear sight, intuition, imagination, wisdom, higher truth, subtle perception, psychic gifts, intellect, logic, intelligence, dream states, and subconscious connection
3. Herbs, plants, and essential oils: Tulsi, Passionflower, Cardamom, Mugwort, Sage, Rosemary, and Holy Basil... Essential oils: Clary Sage, Sandalwood, Marjoram, Rosemary, Patchouli, Frankincense, and Juniper

Crown Chakra

Your Crown chakra is the seventh major chakra that awakens and opens when all of your other chakras are in a state of harmony and flow. Your Crown chakra is located at the top of your head and connects with your Root through kundalini energy. Your serpent-like power or kundalini energy symbolizes sensuality, creative life force, sexual energy, psychic instincts, spiritual powers, and intuition. Your Crown chakra represents cosmic consciousness, faith, hope, inspirational qualities, a cord with the divine, higher perspectives, quantum and spiritual laws, and interconnectedness; the Divine plan of oneness. Past, present, and future lives come in here. Higher truth and wisdom connected to astral vision, ethereal wisdom, and ancient knowledge trickle down through the soul planes to reach your Crown chakra. In terms of kundalini, your essential life force needs a full circuit to perpetually charge/energize and soothe/harmonize your other chakras. Your Crown symbolizes mystical, transcendental, and other worldly experiences- the sublime, divine, and everything above and beyond the 3D human timeline experience. Seeing through the veil of illusion is linked here. Also, artistic, musical, and creative inspiration and unlocking your inner creative genius!

As the kundalini or serpent-like sexual energy flows from root to crown, this chakra ultimately is responsible for the types of sexual experiences you attract in your life. If the Crown is closed, then you are not able to see from a higher awareness, moreover your intuition and perception may be clouded and your emotions "muddied." This blocks you from true love, soulmate connections, and intimate bonds, as well as the capacity you have to discern coupled with making the right decisions in life. Healing your Crown chakra is paramount for a complete, harmonized, and holistic mind, body, & spirit system, in addition to healing your shadow traits and finding enlightenment. It is only once you have created wholeness and harmony within that you can truly be a gift for others, shining and reflecting your beautiful light out to the world. The associated colors are white, violet, and clear/transparent with golden-light as an additional healing quality. The associated element is superconsciousness.

Ways to work with your Crown chakra

1. Crystal therapy: Clear Quartz, Selenite, Sapphire, Ruby, Sugilite, Diamond, Celestie, Angelite, and White Howlite
2. Daily mantra keyword focus: Cosmic consciousness, faith, purity, hope, inspiration, intuition, clairvoyance, divine perception, spirituality, mysticism, and multidimensionality
3. Herbs, plants, and essential oils: Gotu Kola, Blue Lotus, Lavender, Angelica, St John's Wort, Mugwort, Iris, Cosmos, California Poppy, and Yarrow... Essential oils: Cedarwood, Lavender, Neroli, Frankincense, Sage, and Palo Santo

A Meditation to Heal & Unblock Your Chakras

Now you are familiar with your chakras and what they correspond to and symbolize, you can incorporate this exercise into daily life. This is a foundation meditation, which can be expanded to a number of other meditation and visualization healing activities. This foundation meditation is excellent for over-emotionalism, hyper-sensitivity, and getting to the root of any block, imbalance, ailment, or internal distortion. Shadow toxic traits can also be soothed and released or embodied and integrated (for holistic and balanced living). Weak boundaries, codependency, and people-pleasing can be overcome, as well as self-sacrifice, low moods, depressive and isolated tendencies, a lack of joy and fire, and the inability to assert or express yourself directly and/or with authority. Additionally, all of your light attributes and gifts can be fine-tuned and integrated.

Creating A Sacred Space

For any meditation or healing activity you will want to create a sacred space. Palo santo, incense, sage, or a resin-like frankincense, or essential oils, can be burned to cleanse and clear your personal space (your aura and the room you will be performing the meditation in). You should keep lighting to a minimum, turn off all artificial lighting, light candles, and/or keep the curtains open for natural sun or moon light. You can alternatively use a himalayan salt lamp or eco lamp. If you're into crystal healing, make sure your crystals are cleansed and charged and place them around you in a circle. (Or choose one to hold in synergy with the chakra you're wanting to unblock or activate.) If you have a shrine or altar, make sure it's cleansed too. Music is the final component of the sacred space set up. You may want to play binaural beats, nature sounds, or put on a tribal drumming track. You can play the OM-ing chant/sound mantra or Tibetan singing bowls, bells, and chimes. All of these can be found free on Youtube or purchased as cd's. For healing with the elements, you can place an item representing each in front of you. For fire, consider a candle, for earth use a gemstone, rock, or crystal, for air choose a feather, and for water a picture of the ocean, a shell, or a bowl of water blessed with a prayer. For spirit/ether, consider an image of a deity or spiritual figure you're inspired by, or an ancestor or Archangel you're familiar with. You can also call on a spirit guide or spirit animal for divine assistance...

- To begin, create your sacred space, close your eyes, and focus on your breath. Take some deep breaths, become conscious of your body. Feel the blood flowing through you, the chi circulating around your whole energetic system, and the ground beneath you. Sync your breath to a calm and steady rate and become peaceful within, aware of your surroundings.

- Bring your hands up to your heart and rub them together slightly. Start to energize your palms. Bring them together facing each other in front of your heart but not touching. Now imagine a ball of glowing light growing between your palms. The color is the associated chakra you are working on... Keep your focus on your breath while simultaneously observing this ball of loving light grow and expand. Set your intention and project it into the healing ball.
- Set your intention on receiving, developing, and increasing the qualities you wish to heal and integrate. For example, if your glowing light is green, you can focus your intent on empathy, kindness, and self-love. If it is blue, the characteristics could be calmness of being, perfect communication, and peaceful expression. Etc.
- Visualize your chosen qualities grow inside the expanding ball of energy. Really *feel* them there, allowing yourself to feel their presence. It's one thing to understand intellectually, but as an empath it's essential to feel and experience.
- Finally, once you feel a connection with both the qualities and the color, slowly bring your ball of light up to the associated chakra. Keep it there for a few moments, continuing to energize it with your intentions and own healing abilities. Then, when you're ready, pour it over you. Visualize it spilling into you and filling your chakra and physical body with these beautiful qualities. Don't rush it, make a connection on an energetic level and breathe deeply into this unique sensation.
- Healing light and vibrations fill you. They pour into your being, allowing the qualities and source essence to unblock, activate, energize, soothe, and balance (your chakra or linked physical body part).
- End the exercise by rubbing your hands together to close the circuit. Rest your hands on your knees in a meditative position, perhaps performing a mudra if you're experienced. Slowly come into your body allowing yourself to feel all the various sensations and emotions arising.

This is a foundation meditation that can be expanded upon! For example, incorporating crystals, future self visualization, or releasing and cord cutting. More of this later.

Color Healing for the Empath Soul

Similar to chakra healing, colors emit unique frequencies that can be worked with for healing and integration. Hopefully this will enhance your journey back to inner peace, harmony, and alignment with your path and purpose. To make it easier to navigate, I have ordered it in synergy with the chakra system.

Black: Black is the color of grounding, protection, and security. Black offers stability, security, and a powerful life force to your healing endeavors. It links to the earth, to how you form roots with yourself, your physical surroundings, and your relationships. It has shielding and protective effects, as well as being linked to mystery, transformation, and magic. Black can increase feelings of safety, inner strength, and physical stamina, moreover emotional and psychological balance. Black opens you up to deeper mysteries of Self and the universe, inner depth, and introspection. It can help with shadow work, feeling more serene, peaceful, and quiet, and tranquility, in addition to helping you to make sense of your inner darkness. Furthermore, black can be used in coming to terms with loss, grief, and death, like a death of a pet or loved one. Black is a cord to deeper spiritual mysteries, the Unknown, and everything hidden, repressed, or unseen, including the unconscious.

Negative qualities to watch out for (use less black): Interest in black magic or the dark arts, evil/mean-spirited thoughts, seduction, emotional detachment or aloofness, depression, pessimism, secretiveness, and seeking power control over others.

Brown: Brown is a deeply earthing and grounding color that helps with all aspects of plant care, gardening, and Mother Earth maintenance. If you're an Environmental empath or enjoy working outdoors on the land, brown will amplify your passion coupled with your ability to engage in healing activities related to Mother Earth. Strength, reliability, resilience, dependability, security, safety, and comfort in your body and the physical environments you find yourself in are part of brown's healing qualities. You can work with this color to overcome feelings of loneliness, sadness, and isolation, in addition to emptiness, a lack of passion or discipline, and decreased devotion in your life. Brown amplifies service to Mother Earth, can increase feelings of security and acceptance in your body if you happen to be plus-sized or of a larger physique, and can remind you of the importance and beauty of sensuality. Fertility is amplified. Sophisticated, honest, protective, and ancient wisdom, and down-to-earth qualities increase.

Negative qualities to watch out for (use less brown): Boredom, simplicity, dullness, predictability, excess routine, isolation, and shyness or reservation.

Red: Positive qualities include passion, vitality, love, romance, libido, sexual life force, self-preservation, prestige, attraction, allure, intimacy, chemistry, self-control, discipline, devotion, energy, adventure, courage, motivation, self-leadership, charisma, and drive. Red can be used to increase any and all of these characteristics. Red stimulates, ignites passion, helps with high or low blood pressure, enhances instincts, amplifies the senses, and can increase dominance, direct communication, and action if you're lacking in these, or are too submissive, passive, or receptive. Associated with blood, red can enhance life force, personal power, and openness to marriage or commitment in love.

Negative qualities to watch out for (use less red): Lust, aggression, dominance, obsession, competition, anger, explosive reactions, unconscious triggers, impulsiveness, impatience, and irritability.

Orange: Orange is amazing for optimism, energy, positivity, warmth, sociability, youthfulness, creativity, happiness, emotional intelligence, vulnerability, and sensitivity. Orange symbolizes emotional depth, maturity, and wisdom, as well as friendships, relationships, and interpersonal exchanges of all types. Orange can be used to heal and soothe your nervous system, in addition to your immune and muscular systems. It's excellent for working through hyper-sensitvities, over-emotionalism, or a lack of or excess of sexual energy. Creative and artistic blocks can be overcome, as well as a lack of sensuality. Orange brings motivation to projects, enhanced self-worth and self-esteem, and vitality. Enthusiasm, excitement, and courage increase, while desire can be amplified. Further, orange is a natural antidepressant that can stimulate joy, independence, originality, innovation, and forgiveness.

Negative qualities to watch out for (use less orange): Impulsiveness, sexual wounds and blocks or hypersexuality, repressed emotions or chaotic emotions, disloyalty, deceit, and triggers birthed from anger, sadness, and pain.

Yellow: Yellow is excellent for optimism, positivity, confidence, self-esteem, and self-worth. Self-empowerment, charisma, and a sunny disposition all come with yellow's healing powers. Yellow helps with depression, a lack of ambition or motivation, drive, enthusiasm, and self-expression. It's ideal for all matters of career, professional pathways, and purpose, like alignment with your true soul's mission, destiny, or legacy. Joy, warmth, charm, soul alignment, creativity, zest, inspiration, and happiness increase with yellow. It can be used for solar plexus healing, enlightenment, personal transformation, and awakening, as well as refinding your true north, authenticity, and deepest passions. Spirituality, nobility, and courage increase, in addition to prosperity, good fortune, and wealth. Yellow is ideal for manifestation, attracting luck, love, and money, and career, service, or vocation enhancement. Other key qualities include self-authority, willpower, radiance, intellectual power, self-control, efficiency, organization, and sense of humor. Logic, wit, gut feelings, nobility, integrity, and an angelic saintlike energy, in some cultures. Its energy is stimulating, warming, and energizing. Yellow can help with a lack of independence, dormant gifts and talents, depression, pessimism, lone wolf syndrome, and social anxiety.

Negative qualities to watch out for (use less yellow): Over-excitability, forceful will, seeking authority over others, too much zest, and idealism.

Green: Green increases renewal, fertility, growth, self-development, and emotional intelligence. It enhances empathy, tolerance, patience, understanding, wisdom, kindness, generosity, and selflessness. Positive feelings, warmth, heart chakra intelligence, a connection with nature, Mother Earth healing, and self-respect amplify. Healing, self-care, and self-love are part of green's healing symbolism and powers. Unconditional love coupled with universal compassion expand, while all qualities of the Heart chakra get a boost with green. Good health, wellbeing, and harmony come with green's healing qualities. Visionary and idealistic qualities expand. Green is an all-rounder the color of balance, wholeness, and integration. Higher truth, power, and wisdom, moreover multidimensional awareness comes with green. Green as symbolic of the Heart chakra is a bridge or cord between lower and higher self. Green harmonizes the mind, body, and spirit, and the emotional, psychological, physical, and spiritual planes. Green represents empathy, morals, and charity in high levels. Also, reliability, responsibility, service, humility, modesty, and a down-to-earth nature increase.

Negative qualities to watch out for (use less green): Envy, greed materialism, hyper-emotionalism, too much emphasis on feelings and instincts *or* logic and intellect (a lack of balance and harmony), spiritual disconnection, and with a lack of green, grief, stagnation, and boredom (that need to be let go of).

Light blue: Light sky or sea blue brings the qualities of peace, serenity, tranquility, stillness of mind, intellect, logic, wit, higher reasoning, and clear sight or perception. Subtle perception, problem-solving, and imagination increase. Light blue enhances positivity, sociability, angelic and divine contact and communication, and avenues to deep wisdom and truth. It is a very harmonious and tranquil color to work with. Purity, a respect for silence and stillness, contemplation, reflection, introspection, and healing come with light blue's energy. Light blue instills calmness, contentment, beauty, relaxation, and appreciation for rest, peace, and sleep. It helps with nervous tension, stress, and anxiety, in addition to seeing higher spiritual perspectives, truth, and the ability to go with the flow. There's a sense of striving for excellency with light blue, finding excitement, passion, and self-mastery in your service, vocation, or creativity. You can find your purpose, align with your true path, and create a legacy; light blue connects with the sea and sky, which both have a lot of unique qualities.

The sea symbolizes depth, beauty of the soul, subconscious wisdom, the imagination, ethereal and astral wisdom, cosmic and spiritual consciousness, the divine, sacred knowledge, and all feminine qualities linked to the water element. The sky is connected to the air element and represents logic, cerebral gifts, higher analytical reasoning, wit, intellect, truth, wisdom, fame, prestige, independence, freedom, liberation, and self-sovereignty.

Negative qualities to watch out for (use less light blue): Too trusting, to easygoing and adaptability, too much peace without a love of drama or a fighting spirit (where necessary),

Dark blue: Dark blue brings integrity, nobility, and a majestic feel and essence. It is amazing for increasing personal power, authority, and majesty, moreover deep wisdom, self-healing, and ancient knowledge. Spirituality, inspiration, self-acceptance, forgiveness, hope, faith, universal consciousness, appreciation, and sacredness come with dark blue's healing powers. Intuition, inner peace, and connection with the Great Spirit and Source increase. Mental, spiritual, and emotional healing can be found. Cleansing, clearing, and releasing karmic cycles come about with dark blue. Fine-tuned perception and intention too. Awareness of your eternal and infinite nature expands and amplifies; dark blue connects you to timeless wisdom, truth, and patience.

Negative qualities to watch out for (use less dark blue): Too much soul and depth and not enough grounding or practical awareness. Dark blue encourages being in touch with life's deeper meanings and mysteries, which comes naturally to you anyway.

Indigo/Purple: Indigo and purple can increase *all* the qualities of the *Third Eye*. This color range expands intuition, subtle perception, access to dream states, inner peace, solitude, contemplation, higher self guidance, clairvoyance, and visionary sight. They enhance justice, universal consciousness, and the bridge between worlds-multidimensionality, purification, and soul alignment. Purple and indigo increase prophecy, subconscious wisdom, and the cord to the divine. Meditation, serenity, and deep levels of self-awareness and consciousness amplify, while the ability to read auras and tune into spiritual energy increase. Service to natural beauty, planetary consciousness and mankind are part of indigo's healing symbolism. Refer to the Third Eye chakra for deeper understanding and guidance on how these colors can heal.

Negative qualities to watch out for (use less purple): A lack of Root and Sacral energy or too much focus on psychic gifts, prophetic vision, and spiritual perspectives. Perhaps aim for less "head in the clouds" energy in daily life! Using color healing to counteract purple is great for when you've become too lost in fantasy, spirituality, or mysticism.

White: White is the color of purity, innocence, and faith, moreover intuition, clairvoyance, and cosmic consciousness. White is purifying, cleansing, and clearing. It sparks higher consciousness and idealism. It stimulates self-healing abilities, kundalini energy, and divinity. White can be used for all aspects of Crown chakra healing. This color rejuvenates innocence, vulnerability. Hopefulness, and your connection with your inner child. It can be used in harmony with any other color to energize and add some purity and magic to that color range. Celestial, heavenly, and ethereal energy increases. You can use white for sexual, spiritual, emotional, or psychological healing. It sparks creative genius, imagination, and idealism, in addition to self-protection, self-sovereignty, and inner guidance. Auric shielding, mysticism, and multidimensionality enhance with white's healing powers. The realm of spirit, everything intangible, and integrity, humility, and morality of the highest order. Divine order too. A lack of Root chakra, including survival, self-preservation, and sexual life force or libido can be overcome.

Negative qualities to watch out for (use less white): The same as for indigo- getting lost in the clouds, an excessive amount of mysticism or spirituality, and illusions. Illusions are common with too much white energy.

Gray: Gray is the color to use for sensibility, sophistication, and dependability. Gray increases business acumen, dignity, conservativeness, maturity, and an orderly, organizational, and material nature. It's excellent for when you're wanting to ground your empath talents or gifts into a business, become more professional, and so on. Practicalities, sage-like wisdom, elegance, refinery, and dignity can be integrated. Gray is excellent to work with when you need more structure, routine, or organization in your life; it can counter excessive "go with the flow" or right brain qualities.

Negative qualities to watch out for (use less gray): Indecision, boredom, too much order and structure, depression, pessimism, repressed emotions, a lack of logic and intellect, and excess routine, conservatism, and sensibility.

Kundalini Serpent-Power: The Journey of Wholeness and Completion

As you are aware by now, your mind, body, and spirit are designed to work in harmony. Your thoughts affect your emotions, which in turn affects your physical body and spiritual health. The same is true in reverse; each "body" or system has a profound influence on the others. In Reiki, it is taught that all illness and disease has its origins on the soul planes. In other words, all illness and imbalance begins on the subtle planes of existence. Any major imbalance or distortion on a soul level, in and of your soul body, trickles down into the others. This affects your mental, emotional, physical, and spiritual body, in addition to abilities and powers connected to your astral body. Your soul body is the perfect blueprint of your soul, the highest expression of yourself. Your DNA holds memories and codons of information linked to our soul's ultimate expression. Awakening your kundalini through chakra healing and awareness is key to attaining self-realization, enlightenment, and the awakening of your dormant DNA. Your kundalini is the *unified, whole,* and *balanced* you. Your kundalini is in a state of flow when your chakras are in harmony, balanced, and healed, unblocked and with chi, your essential life force, freely flowing. As an empath, this is the source of your spiritual gifts, intuition, advanced creative and artistic abilities, and so forth. It can therefore be seen that the ultimate goal of the empath is to reach your highest vibratory state, so you can live your best life, achieve self-mastery, and fulfill your soul purpose.

Everything advanced comes into the kundalini. Not all empaths are destined to travel; deep into the spiritual and soul planes. Your legacy might be to help hundreds to thousands of people through unique counseling gifts! Or to soothe the pain and suffering of animals, plant-life, or the elderly. Not every empath is capable of the following, but they are *available* to you. And for those who do have it in their soul's blueprint to evolve and ascend to such heightened frequencies, let's just say you are here to step into a godly, superhuman status. You are a natural healer, as this is what manifests and sparks with an activated kundalini; healing hands, healing presence, and potent mystical and spiritual gifts.

Let's explore some of these themes and abilities now.

1. **Akashic Records**: Your Akashic Records are a complete record of your soul's blueprint, a living library available on the quantum and holographic planes. Akashic Records communicate every memory, relationship, and experience you've ever heard, from a cosmic perspective. From the birth of your soul to this lifetime, all memories are available to you. They can be accessed through conscious fasting, transcendental meditation, plant medicines, astral and visionary insights, and lucid or conscious dreaming. Asking your angels, spirit guides, or the Archangels for assistance can also activate neural pathways to the Akashic Record.
2. **Past, present, and future lives**: Knowledge of past, present, and future lives are closely linked to advanced empath superpowers. You see life and reality

multidimensionally, not linearly like most humans. You understand that we are timeless, eternal, and infinite beings, and that there are multiple planes, dimensions, and frequencies. Access to past, present, and future lives comes with advanced soul-searching, shadow and trauma work/therapy, and self-healing. This is an excellent route and tool to deeper self-discovery, potent transformation, and ascended consciousness.

3. **Soul activation and ascension**: Soul activation and ascension are things you hear nowadays, yet may not be exactly sure what they mean. Your soul activates and awakens through clearing, cleansing, and healing work. This stimulates your innate star seed abilities. Now, star seed gifts and powers is a rather big topic- I could have easily have included a whole chapter on this. From Sirian to Indigo and Pleiadian to Arcturian, many of us who awaken spiritually become aware of advanced cosmic communities and races we are or have been connected to. Personally, I believe all is continued in the one atom, in a single cell of DNA; the macrosmc is the microcosm. This is something you can research in your own time, if you feel like doing so. But, one certain truth to note is: we all come from the stars. Our DNA holds memories, gifts, and knowledge of ancient civilizations, moreover our cosmic connections up above. Food for thought.

4. **Advanced astral abilities**: Lucid dreaming, astral travel, astral projection, and prophetic dreaming... we are gifted and active in the subtle, energetic, and multi-dimensional planes. If you wish to explore this unique topic further, consider studying to become a Dream therapist or Energy worker. Become open to holistic and alternative therapies, shamanic modalities, or the psychic and tarot community. Divination runs in your blood.

5. **Shamanic healing powers**: Many empaths are natural shamans and seers with cords to ancient lineages. I myself got guided to begin studies and pathways aligned to the Munay Ki and Shamanic Reiki lineages. These visions, divine messages, and direct insights began in 2012, in harmony with the 2012 Grand Cycle Shift. You may be a shapeshifter. You may be in tune with spirit animals, guides, and ancestors. You may have experienced deep inner knowing from an early age, which only grows when older.

6. **Natural awareness of psychic attack, cord cutting, and channeling gifts**: Furthermore, we empaths have a natural awareness and affinity with psychic attack, cord cutting, and channeling gifts. These are higher spiritual abilities that extend above and beyond the "normal" mind-reading/deep empathy, emotional intelligence, instincts, intuition, and general psychic gifts. Conscious fasting is a way to access all of the abilities in this list, if you're not into plant medicines (plants and herbs that raise consciousness). Your natural healing hands and healing presence can inspire seer-like qualities that could make you into a world-class psychic, astrologer, tarot reader, healer, shaman, prophet, mystic, or so on. If this is the path you choose...

✧

Chapter 5: Healing, Self-Care, and Personal Discovery

Staying Balanced, Centered, and Aligned

Let's now explore the various tips & techniques, exercises, and self-development activities best for empaths.

Learning to Lighten Up and Laugh

As an empath, it can be very easy to take life too seriously, always choosing to be serious or mellow (when holding space) or serene and peaceful (when embodying an advanced emotional frequency for others). Laughter doesn't come as naturally to many empaths as creating harmony, tranquility, and serenity. Joy and playfulness require some inner fire, and this is somethin empaths tend to lack. To heal, simply make a conscious effort to laugh more. Tell yourself to laugh, program your subconscious mind with the mantra of laughter. Change your self-talk. Tell yourself to laugh more, choose joy and an upbeat energy when presented with different options in social circles. You tend to go for deep, serious, and soul bonding communication and connection. Aligning with an upbeat and joyous energy isn't your first choice, it's not a natural choice for you. One of the main reasons you suffer when around people or out of your comfort zone is due to your *oversensitivity*; there really is no need to be so sensitive or self-conscious all the time. To overcome sensitivity, laugh more. Make it genuine and sincere, not one of those evil or mean-spirited laughs, but a laugh that recognizes we are all one and interconnected. Everyone is your mirror, a reflection of you. Laughing releases trapped emotions, removes blocks to higher perspectives, and connects you to others. Laughter establishes intimacy, as well as depth and bonding. Laughter can help you in many social situations, specifically with bringing trapped energy to conscious light, overcoming social anxiety, and easing tension or insecurities. Laughter moves energy up from the subconscious or unconscious to the conscious. Laughing *shakes things up,* allowing you to see, observe, and get a feel for your own energy. Self-alignment comes about through laughter, and further positive change, transformation, and spiritual illumination increase and occur.

Working With Your Dreams and the Subconscious Mind

Your dreams are a direct gateway and portal to higher consciousness, deep insights, and avenues to self-healing, sacred knowledge, and ancient wisdom. Wisdom and subconscious guidance found in dreams can help you develop stronger boundaries, find your personal truths, and manifest abundance, love, luck, friendship, or opportunities in waking life. There is so much wisdom to be found in dreams. Any issue, block, or imbalance you may be suffering with can be eased on the dreamspace. Your subconscious mind works in harmony with your Higher Self and soul, so secrets, dormant gifts, and hidden information can come to light. There is an infinite sea of knowledge available. Universal symbolism and archetypes can come to conscious light- everything dark or hidden can make its way to the forefront of your conscious mind. You are intelligent on a cellular level, your cells "know," they speak to you. Your intuitive and psychic muscles strengthen and come alive during sleep, specifically REM sleep, where you dream. Dreaming is more than a space to recharge for you, although it is an incredibly powerful space to recharge your soul's light, merging you directly with the Source. It's also a place where you explore multidimensional avenues of knowledge and healing power, so you can be of service in waking life reality. It is in dreams where dormant parts of you spark and awaken, subconsciousness is triggered, which then activates hidden gifts, emotions, and memories.

Another key area of exploration lies in unique dream gifts, like precognitive dreaming, the gift of prophetic sight, and receiving direct wisdom from spirit guides, passed over loved ones, or unique dream characters in the dream space. Here's a real life example: in my youth I had a powerful dream where a fairy godmother type character imparted deep wisdom on me. She told me of a specific herbal supplement a friend needed to help with her irregular and painful periods. Her moon cycles were a bit messed up! And she suffered as a result. This fairy godmother character told me she needed Agnus Castus, a unique herbal remedy for women going through such things. Well, I advised her to take Agnus Castus a few weeks later, and it really helped... it was exactly what she needed.

Dreams are here to serve your healing gifts and powers. They help you serve from the highest source and light, connecting to ancient knowledge, and receiving help from spirit guides and ancestors. Angels and Archangels can visit you in dreams. Powerful beings may appear, giving you vivid imagery, symbolism, and details that help you be a better and more wise and loving channel. You can research natural dream supplements to help with this area of self-development. I've tried *all* of these and have had no problems, but I don't take pharmaceuticals, recreational drugs, or anything similar. My body is a pure channel, in other words, therefore there have been no side effects! Make sure you do efficient research before consuming any of these.

Stronger/more lucid and astrally-enhancing effects:

1. Mugwort
2. Silene Capensis (African Dream Root)
3. 5-HTP
4. Calea Zacatechichi

Milder/subtle sensations of euphoria and astral effects:

5. Chamomile tea
6. Passion flower
7. Lemon Balm
8. Valerian

The Importance of Discernment (A quality I once couldn't pronounce!)

When I made my first video on empathic healing from narcissistic abuse, I couldn't even pronounce the word discernment. It was something I was only just integrating, therefore I couldn't say it (this is how holographic, holistic, and authentic we empaths are- our whole reality is tied into emotions and our interconnectedness!). To discern is to discriminate and judge sophisticatedly and with both logic and intuition. It's sound judgment using a combination of instincts, fine-tuned senses, analytical thinking, higher reasoning, and intellectual understanding merged with holographic or multidimensional thinking. It's seeing the "big picture" with your higher angelic or spiritual eyes intact. Also, with both right brain and left brain qualities being made use of. Discernment is a git many empaths lack earlier in life, mainly due to a lack of intellect, logic, and analytical power. We're very "right brain," signifying we tend to be more intuitive, imaginative, and "free flow" (multidimensional) in thought than scientific, factual, or linear. Without discernment, however, you would be able to ascertain who is for you. Discernment helps with toxic, manipulative, and deceptive characters. It allows you to see the big picture, the whole story, and the larger vision in play. So you can uncover hidden motives, subtle emotions and intentions, and people's true reasons for wanting to connect, have you as a lover, or choose you as a business partner. Not everyone is honest. There are some deceptive characters in this world, and many people further play on the empath heart. You're so innocent! You're so kind, selfless, and caring. Not everyone is worthy of your unconditional love, generosity, and compassion, quite simply. Incorporate discernment and its energetic characteristics into your daily self-care, meditation, or affirmation program. It will work wonders on your self-esteem, as well as your ability to put up- and keep- healthy boundaries.

Next we explore:-

- ❖ Psychic Self-Development
- ❖ Auric Shielding, Healing, and Protection
- ❖ Healing with Crystals
- ❖ How to Create A Chi Ball
- ❖ A unique Tree Grounding Meditation

****

During the creation process, I decided to cut this section out. In the name of transparency, integrity, and authenticity, I felt it wouldn't be fair to my clients, the people I have *ghostwritten* for, to include these here. These are exercises I have shared in a number of books- all with original wording, of course, yet may come across as "repeated information."

I will be creating a course centered around these advanced healing techniques, which will be released in the upcoming years. My apologies for any inconvenience.

Grace Gabriella ✧

Who's Secretly Throwing Rocks In Your Boat?

"Empath burnout" coupled with being drained and depleted by energy vampires, users, takers, and simply ungrateful people who see you as an emotional dumping ground are some of your greatest challenges in life. They're things that keep you stuck and bound, in addition to blocked, stagnant, and chained to negative and karmic cycles. Empaths encounter multiple people throughout their lives who secretly throw rocks in your boat. Your ship is sinking, and you don't know why. You pour your love, energy, and devotion out into the world, yet you only receive hate, indifference, envy, indifference, or coldness back. Why? Well, dear empath, not everyone is on your team. There are secret enemies not routing for you, further trying to bring you down. I am sorry to share this, but it's the truth. I myself have had many people I genuinely considered soul family- people I dreamed about for years upon years, throw rocks in my previous and fragile little boat. (A symbol for how gentle and humble I am.) There are hidden enemies masking as friends and even family. There are people who smile to your face when you're in your native and innocent mental frame, and then laugh, ridicule, and slander you behind your back. Some of your so-called friends even take action against you, by shaming you, throwing shade to your name publicly, or trying to belittle and downgrade you. It's only when you begin to find your worth, lose the extreme naivety, and find some boundaries that you start to see things and people for what they really are.

I am not suggesting everyone's a narcissist or a monster, but not everyone has the empath heart or soul either. Imagine yourself as a ship sailing gracefully across the sea… The ocean and waters of the world are seen to represent our subconscious, the vast and deep, infinite waters where all of our beliefs, identity, thoughts, emotions, and subtle impressions arise. Our emotions are also birthed from water while the subconscious mind is said to be representative of the sea. We enter into relationships, making our own ship just as important. You truly are captain of your own destiny. Your boat- your divine sacred vessel, is significant. So you must keep it in maintenance, keep checking to see if the people in your boat are really on your side. Behind your back, some of your sailors, crew, guests, or even a co-captain may be secretly trying to sink the ship. Why? Well, jealousy, hatred, envy, a separation mindset birthed from society's illusions or addictions, and many other reasons are possible answers. As the captain and master of your ship and destiny, it's your responsibility to make sure everything is in working order. Divine order. Self-care practices and daily rituals that honor your wellbeing are called for. You must put up and maintain healthy boundaries, as this is a true sign of emotional maturity. You can't be everyone's emotional dumping ground or doormat forevermore. Too many holes in your boat or ship and everyone drowns, or the ship sinks entirely. Boundaries not only benefit you, but everyone on your ship, i.e. everyone in your life. All of your connections benefit from having clear and healthy boundaries, so you're not only helping yourself but doing what you love to; being of service to others.

Getting Plenty Of Down Time and Me time

Down time is essentially for you, because to come up and into the light you must first spend time in darkness. Too much time in the light, being sociable, and sharing your gifts and wisdom, and you fall into a polarity. Empaths are not superficial, not in the slightest, and this means you can't operate like many normal people in this world. Mellowness is natural. Spending time alone and in isolation, even being a bit dark and gloomy, is normal. You thrive in darkness, as it makes you appreciate the people in your life more. This is the whole purpose of shadow work; notice when I speak about shadow work, I not only talk about releasing and transcending- letting go of, but *integrating and balancing*. To attain enlightenment, you must embrace and embody your shadow attributes. Remember the yin and yang symbol- dualistic forces flow into one another. Sometimes you will be a light amongst a sea of darkness, shining your beautiful light, and other times you will be darkness in a world of light, taking time to recharge and recenter. Down time, me time, and rest does you the world of good! Introspective activities make your soul glow and shine, you love it. Not many people can get a bit depressive and gloomy and find real solace and comfort there. The secret is: it's your source of wisdom. Self-knowledge, sacred knowledge, and divine truths and inspiration are found in darkness, in the shadow lands and realms. Additionally, subconscious wisdom, guidance, and healing forces are found in darkness. Darkness is a powerful tunnel back to the light.

Rest and down time aren't just linked to shadow work and integration. You can find real comfort in your solitude, in being a lone wolf. If we take this saying and delve a little deeper, we will see that the *Wolf spirit animal symbolism* relates to instincts, amazing intuition and senses, powerful extrasensory gifts, and a love of solitude and community bonds. Wolves symbolize both solitude and independence and society, family, and community bonds in equal measure. Wolves are telepathically in tune too, so it's no wonder this saying applies to empaths.

Your energy is powerful, while your emotions and mood influence everyone around you. Your subtle intentions, feelings, and thoughts radiate outwards to affect the overall mood and "vibe" of a room, gathering, or physical environment. You are a powerful shaper and creator of your world, so you need time to rest, recharge, and gather wisdom and knowledge. Spend time alone; eat alone, meditate, go for nature walks, watch inspiring documentaries, read, or simply *be* and relax with your favorite music. We are human beings... not human doings. Invisible energy is real, it permeates all living things. To maintain such advanced emotional and spiritual frequencies, you must go inside yourself and take down/me time every once and awhile. Due to your giving, selfless, and unconditionally loving empathic nature, you frequently find yourself depleted in energy. Excessive social interactions and situations drain you, you pick up on every subtle impression around you. You are the fuel to everyone's fire... And this means you can either bring the vibe down or lift it up. You're powerful, and this is not being spoken from ego. If you want to make real change, be of service, and inspire everyone, touching the hearts of the people you meet, it's important to make peace with your darkness. It's ok to be a bit moody! It's ok to need down time, to do your own thing, and to say "no" to others with your time and energy. It's not only ok, but it's perfectly natural, empath.

If ever in doubt, repeat this mantra:

"By giving quality time to myself, I am better able to give my time and energy to others. My sensitivities are a strength and a superpower, but only when channeled wisely and in harmony with my own best interests. My wishes, needs, and desires matter. Self-care is essential for my wellbeing. Self- love is not selfish, nor is it bad... When I give myself space to shine I allow others to do the same. We are all one and interconnected, and this means I should put myself first sometimes, to be the best divine channel and healing light for others."

You Can't Be Brilliant Without Boundaries, Dear One

Boundaries is your new power word! Being an empath is hard due to your heightened sensitivity and higher frequency emotional connection and functioning. One of your main issues in life, therefore, is to develop and make friends with the word boundaries. It may be difficult at first, especially due to your innate desire to be "everyone's friend in need" and help others in some way; yet, as you know, this leaves you drained and lacking in energy, vitality and wellbeing. One of the key pieces of wisdom to be aware of when learning about your boundaries is the recent discoveries of neuroscience and quantum physics. Neuroscientists and quantum physicists have found that we are in fact governed by an aura, an electromagnetic energy field which emits, transmits, and receives thoughts, emotions, and subtle impressions. Our auras- or electromagnetic fields- interact with others, and this is not just limited to other humans. Every living thing from plants to flowers and crystals or rocks have an auric field. This means we essentially *converse* with others on a subtle level in every moment of now. This has some profound implications. Emotions, subtle energy and unique spiritual-energetic gifts define empathy, therefore being aware of the power of your own being can be heaven or hell- literally. This is where boundaries come into play.

As you will see later narcissists and other toxic personalities are magnets to your vibe. They simply love your energy, love, compassion, and inner beauty but not in a healthy way. This means that having healthy boundaries and centeredness is *essential*. One of the most effective things you can do is to engage in aura strengthening and developing exercises and activities.

✧

Chapter 6: Shadow Work, Root Exploration, and the Empath Subconscious

Your Shadow Self: The *Root* to Healing and Wholeness

As briefly mentioned earlier, your traumas and ancestral wounds are issues that have grown with you since childhood. They are the *subconscious* and *repressed* aspects of yourself that are brought into adult relationships, when unchecked and unhealed. Traumas and wounds run deep because they are often connected to the relationships we keep, from early family bonds to friends, partners, and lovers. This implies that we get hurt quite easily, being sensitive and prone to hyper-emotionalism. We also take on the world's suffering, which means we have both our own and the collective's, or planetary healing, to deal with. Empaths have access to the collective psyche, in addition to the over-soul. The over-soul is the planetary soul, the one planetary consciousness whereby all individual consciousness streams. Shadow work and shadow integration are essential for wholeness and self-mastery, but to achieve this we must go deep into the subconscious mind. To suggest only empaths are capable of depth or unconditional love and compassion would be ignorant. This is not what this topic implies. However, it is true that empaths are deeper than a lot of people in this world. It's our core programming, our authentic vibration. We empaths tend to absorb people's personal traumas, stories, and wounds, at least certainly before we've implemented proper boundaries. Everyone has a unique soul print, a specific story and frequency; empaths care so much that it becomes a life mission to heal virtually everyone you come across. This isn't realistic, sane, or sustainable, however, so to truly heal and be an amazing being of service for the collective, you must work on yourself. It all begins with yourself.

You are all too familiar with the struggles that come with being an empath. Growing up, you may have been called too sensitive, shy, or labeled as odd or crazy. You may have been taunted, bullied, or teased. You may have been brought up in oppressive structures or regimes contrary to your empathic nature, with parents, teachers, or elders attempting to impose irrational or unjustifiable belief systems on you. You were certainly misunderstood, the "oddball" or "black sheep." Your unique gifts and abilities may not have been seen or appreciated due to growing up in a masculine and extroverted world. This brings us onto **The Wound of the Soul**. *The Wound of the Soul* can be split into two distinct parts: Childhood Wounds and the Shadow Self.

Let's explore these now.

Childhood Wounds

Based on the faulty and misinformed information given as a child, you developed a core childhood wound. This could manifest as any of the following:-

1. Feeling scared or unable to express your emotions, feelings, and unique perspectives. You developed a fear of expression, communication, and using your voice.
2. Feeling scared or unable to be creative, artistic, or imaginative. There were limits put on your creativity and freedom of expression. Your colorful, fun-loving, and playful self was suppressed as a result.
3. Feeling scared or unable to come out of your shell, be more friendly and warm, and be the life and soul of the party, in any way. You were always blocked by parents, teachers, or peers just as you were ready to stop being so shy and withdrawn.

Holistically speaking, society doesn't support empaths. We encourage calculated, logical, sporty, fiery, and energetic people. This is due to society being patriarchal, at present. Patriarchy is symbolic of masculine energy, and masculine energy represents air and fire; the mind, intellect, and logic, and competition, sport, and physical strength. Emotional and spiritual strength- feminine gifts, aren't generally considered strong to mainstream education, traditional business models, or the patriarchal society we currently reside in. Fire and air are masculine/yang, while earth and water are feminine/yin. Empathy is a feminine gift, but society is currently operating from masculine principles. So, you can see where the problem is.

This creates a divide in the empath psyche, leading to many core wounds and traumas that come into adulthood. Being feeling based, emotional, and sensitive has its downfalls. We're not yet living in conscious or spiritual communities where our unique gifts are encouraged and supported. The empath nature and all associated qualities are actually overlooked, ridiculed, and dismissed- fiery, cerebral, and extroverted types tend to put out our light, stomp over us, or gaslight us into silence and submission. *True story.*

Quick Disclaimer:

Being an empath is not synonymous with your Astrological star sign. Yes, the empath blueprint is very closely tied into the elements, yin and yang theory, and universal energies and principles. *But* this doesn't mean all fire and air signs are narcissistic or non-empaths, nor that all earth and water signs are empaths. There is more to astrology than your sun sign. A fire sign may have a potent water Moon placement... Equally, a water or earth sign might have some significant air or fire placements. For example, you could be an egotistical and self-entitled Aries (Aries' shadow) with a beautifully balanced, serene, and compassionate Cancer Moon. Simultaneously, you could be an empathic, unconditionally loving, and selfless Pisces with a Leo Moon, something that, philosophically, would make you less of an empath (if judging the empath scale purely based on astrology). The combinations are vast.

Thus, in school, the norm is to be loud, confident, and expressive. Also, rational, logical, and scientific- left brain. Being artistic, creative, and intuitive are almost seen as some "extracurricular" activity. (Even writing this made me laugh out loud.) The moral of the story is: you almost certainly suffered unjust, unfair, and ill-treatment, possibly on a minor level but likely majorly. Empaths are like dolphins out of water or sloths stranded in the middle of a road... As you know empathy is defined by a rich imagination, advanced emotional wisdom and connection, and a tendency towards deep, authentic, and real connection. As an empath, you may thrive in solo activities or one-to-one communications, also enjoying introspective activities as described earlier (like gardening, reading, spending time in nature, expressing yourself in solitude through art or music, and so on). You also may be an original thinker, a philosopher at heart, or possess a deeply inventive and creative mind. Finally, you may have had a sense of spiritual knowing and were drawn to unexplainable phenomena. All of these can be suppressed, ridiculed, and down-played in Western society. Because children require the support, care, and loving guidance from grown-ups, not having this left you deepl uncentered and ungrounded. You were like a boat lost at sea without an anchor or captain, getting pulled around by multiple currents.

The Shadow Self and *The Wound of the Soul*

The Shadow Self is one of Carl Jung's *universal archetypes*, and I've chosen to share it here to show its significance. The shadow self is part of yourself that you have hidden, suppressed, or rejected. It's the parts of you you deny or dismiss, due to fear of judgment, insecurity, abuse, misdirection, or faulty information presented to you. In terms of the empath nature, your shadow self is linked to the "empath collective psyche." This is, essentially, truths specific to all empaths. The famous psychiatrist and one of the founding fathers of modern psychology, Carl Jung, came up with a set of *universal archetypes* to define the whole self. These universal archetypes are inherent within all human beings and often appear as symbols in dreams. For empaths, the shadow self is particularly useful for healing and self-exploration work.

Let's look at some of the shadow aspects to being an empath:

Suppression of Intimacy and Connection

Despite your innate longing for connection and intimacy, moreover intimate bonding, one of your downfalls is being closed off to deep and meaningful bonding. This is due to fear because you feel so deeply. You could be the most physically beautiful, slim or curvaceous as a woman, muscular or toned as a man, and flawlessly skin, face, and hair perfect human; all empaths are scared to love and be loved. You are so deep, genuine, and sincere in your emotions and desires. Your affections are true, the compliments you give are real. You live, speak, and act from the heart, even when you're flirting or showing your sexually liberated side. Empaths are real lovers with diamond souls. So this is a difficult area. You tend to suppress your romantic, intimate, and sexual needs. It can be hard for you to fully open up and merge with someone on a deep level, as you're scared of being hurt. You love quickly and get hurt easily, you're fragile and sensitive. If or when the bond breaks, you tend to withdraw into your shell. If in youth you've made many bad choices, having your heart broken, having given your all in love, you can expect to find your heartbreak leading to suppression and a breakdown of intimacy. Sexual repression can take over, as well as blocks to self-love, romance, and general openness and vulnerability in sexual relationships.

Lack of Self-Love

Due to needing to be everyone's empath or everyone's free healer, therapist, and counselor, you can choose to sacrifice your needs to the point of a lack of self-love, self-care, and diminished boundaries. Over time, this leads to resentment, feelings of being used and taken advantage of, and low self-worth. Your self-esteem suffers, which makes you shy and lacking confidence in a social setting, where or when you're supposed to be shining your light and sharing your gifts with others. In terms of wounds and your soul, a lack of self-love prevents you from finding your flow, establishing family or community bonds, and living in harmony with your soul mission, purpose, or true path. A lack of self-love prevents true intimacy, companionships, and partnerships, creative, professional, or romantic, from flowing. You become stuck, blocked, and stagnant, fixated on helping others without realizing that you still have healing to do. Shadow work suffers, you become idealistic and fantastical in your notions and beliefs in love and friendship, yet never take the real or practical steps to get there. You have a powerful vision, being idealistic and visionary minded, but you don't find your authentic truth, voice, or power, until later in life. Your key to overcoming childhood wounds and collective trauma is to accept the reality of life's experiences and situations. Be more realistic, practical, and material-minded. Try not to get lost in fantasies or ideals. Grounding is highly significant for you, as is paying attention to details.

If we take a quick glance at astrology, with Pisces being the sign of the empath, we can see what your key lessons are. Virgo is Pisces' opposite sign, and the whole point of astrology is to find balance and harmony with your opposite sign. Pisces the empath and old soul is mystical, spiritual, selfless, caring, nurturing, sweet, submissive, and deeply compassionate, all qualities of the empath nature. Virgo, Pisces' opposite, lacks vision as well as big picture seeing, but is very practical, responsible, and methodological. They're intellectual, logical, and modest with a down-to-earth nature. They help you to see the importance of the small details, moreover being a perfectionist and analytical to connect to the practical elements of life. You can find inspiration in the Virgo sign to ground, balance, and heal on levels you may have previously thought you didn't need healing. Many empaths don't think they need to be more practical or grounded- your duty is to bring an evolved emotional frequency into the world, right? Wrong, well, not entirely accurate. Even if you end up finding someone dominant and being in a loving nurturing relationship (where your submissive side can come out), you still need to pay attention to the smaller details. Not everything is about big picture vision or prophetic and divine insights.

The Simple Life

Heard of divine simplicity? I'm sure you have. Empaths love the simple life, are all about divine simplicity, and seem to be attracted to more quiet and mellow types. You can't find your happy place when you're constantly seeking external things, chasing distractions, and trying to fit in with the crowd. Related to needing a quiet, humble, and divinely simplistic life is feeling you need to put on hold your talents or ambitions, for example, being overly selfless to the point of self-sacrifice. (A key lifelong theme for you.) The faulty belief that you're not allowed to be successful, famous, or financially abundant is rooted in poverty consciousness, and poverty consciousness stems from childhood wounds. Trauma is buried deep within your psyche, a direct manifestation of a lack of love, care, and empathy growing up. When teachers, parents, or guardians don't give us empaths what we need, we repress our emotions and feelings. We feel unable to express our deepest needs, moreover our heart's desires, opinions, beliefs, wants, emotions, and so forth. Because we begin to witness everyone else being colorful, playful, fun-loving, and expressive, also receiving what they need (from society, which supports air/cerebral and physical/sporty types), we start to break down inside. We become numb to our true feelings and deepest emotions.

We believe that we should live in poverty consciousness, like we're not worthy of prosperity, security, and loving support. This has been hammered into our psyches through endless neglect, dismissal, and misunderstood needs and behaviors. Thus, we suppress our need to make money, have savings, be practical, receive security, and receive from others; we become mistaken, thinking we need to give, suffer, or over-share. You suffer from the belief that you must live in constant service to others, whether it be animals, people, or the planet. But, life is supposed to be a healthy flow of giving and receiving; personal successes, joys, and pleasures should be embraced. Empaths are downtrodden, treated as doormats, and very much neglected in childhood, youth, and even young adults. People don't understand our complex emotional needs nor our sensitivities. This creates a core wound associated with the inner child... we don't know how to ask for help, receive the love we need, or express our talents, wisdom, or most authentic feelings later in life.

Blocks to Physical Health and Well-Being

Due to an overly yin and watery nature, empaths tend to develop blocks to physical health and fitness. We focus so much on the emotional and spiritual aspects of life. We put all of our time and energy into emotional self-mastery, spiritual gift development, and being a loving healer, helper, and caregiver for others. As a result, we neglect physical health and well-being. Sport doesn't come naturally to us, in fact, empaths are usually the ones picked last or second to last in school sports games! Many empaths either don't feel the need to engage in fitness regimes and sport, or overlook their importance altogether. The empath blueprint is defined by soul, sensitivity, emotional vulnerability, feelings, spiritual gifts, etc. strenuous sport and solely physical body focus don't really come into this. Because you're so busy taking care of everyone else and all of their needs, physical care is a secondary, tertiary, or even last thought, or a non-existent one.

Escapism

Like Pisces, the astrological sign of the empath, you are a master escapist, or you have been at some point in your life. Escapism is the desire to escape when reality gets too cold or harsh for you. Relationships, situations, environments, places, and people make you feel shy and scared inside. You feel disconnected, while secretly being more connected to everyone's feelings and emotions than anyone else. This creates a nervous and anxious individual who resorts to drugs, addictive behaviors, or escapism as a coping mechanism. You run away, get lost in your feelings, or become super-empathic to the point of absorbing absolutely everything around you. You're like a boat lost out at sea, dear empath. It's difficult, life itself can be heartbreaking; you may be someone who can't leave a single snail on the sidewalk when they're out of the bushes. You may cry with complete strangers or take on the pain of an animal, no matter how great or small. Escapism occurs when you've lacked boundaries, moreover have existed primarily in your emotional body for too long. Escapism is linked to addictions and the victim-martyr-savior complex.

Addictions

Food, tobacco, drug, sex, porn, substance, television, or any other addiction can manifest. Over time, addictive behaviors and mindsets become habitual. They integrate into your personality and in turn restructure DNA, which changes the empath blueprint entirely! Empaths tend to develop addictions when we've been out of tune with our bodies for too long. Denial or rejection of essential physical needs- exercise, sex, intimacy, the right foods, and self-care routines, can make us resort to other fixes. Pisces is ruled by Neptune, the planet of psychic instincts, spirituality, and mysticism (positive empath traits), but also escapism, fantasy, and illusions (negative empath traits). You can become addicted to any of the above, as well as lost in the realm of fantasies and illusions. These are either created by you or created by others. Addictions prevent healing, shadow work, and alignment with your true path and community. Selfless service is prevented with addictions, yet they seem to be the perfect empath escape. Your goal to self-mastery is to recognize where and when you may have been disassociated too long. Discord, disconnection, and distortion rule a young empath's life.

The Victim-Martyr-Savior Complex

Finally, the victim-martyr-savior complex is a very prominent aspect to the shadow side of an empath. This refers to the feeling of being a victim followed by believing one needs to take on martyrdom or a savior role. This sparks a painful and self-detrimental cycle. You may be a victim, at least when examining how you are prey to a lot of predatory characters. But, playing victim is another story because this takes away from your personal power. Then, the cycle of trying to be everyone's savior or a martyr initiates. This only limits you and your growth more. This triangle can last for years to decades, it all depends on what's included in your healing journey in your soulprint. Luckily, recognizing it is the first step to healing it.

The Wound of the Soul

The wound of the soul is the part of your soul that has been carried throughout lifetimes. This means that you have experienced many lifetimes where in each you have brought lessons with you into the next. You finally reach your current stage of evolution and self- empowerment in this life with all of the lessons and teachings intact. They are part of your unique soulprint, *soul's blueprint*. As an empath, you have gone through many tests, trials, and tribulations that have made you stronger, more intuitive, and much more wise. Your core soul wound is a block to your highest expression, Higher Self, and ultimate soul's purpose and alignment. All of your talents, wisdom, and gifts only become activated when you've started to work on your wounds and trauma.

Carl Jung's Universal Archetypes

Carl Jung was a famous Swiss psychiatrist and one of the founders of modern psychology. He came up with a set of *universal archetypes* of *the Self*, which are aspects of the whole human being, relating to everyone on earth. Regardless of culture, race, identity, gender, sexuality, religion, or color, every human has these universal archetypes within. These archetypes were created from his explorations of the collective unconscious, through different religions of the East and West, as well as mythology and alchemy. He further advocated that these archetypes manifest themselves in dreams through symbols and figures. Once activated, they could unlock a specific frequency or energy type within the person, specifically associated with the archetype. When exploring what it means to be an empath, I believe it is essential to look to the *subconscious aspects* of ourselves for wholeness, full understanding, healing, self-evolution, and integration. Carl Jung's archetypes are here to inspire and educate us. They explain how and why we operate, how we can heal, and what could be missing for happy and peaceful living. Our brains are transmitters and receivers of consciousness; it's in dreams where we learn a great deal about our impressions, emotions, and beliefs, as well as gaining insight and wisdom for everyday reality.

Let's now explore each of the universal archetypes and how they relate to the wonderful gift of empathy.

The Persona

The persona is the image you present to the world in daily life. It is your mask, public persona, and image that you want others to see you as. For example, the caring empath, the inventive scientist, the nurturing mother, the ambitious leader, or the gifted musician. The term persona literally comes from the Latin "mask," in dreams it is represented by *the Self*, a character you know is you. Jung referred to the persona as the conformity archetype, and believed it essential in personal development. Depending on where you are at in your own journey of transformation, empaths often feel they have to put on a mask, be something for everyone, and play certain roles. This is of course rooted in people-pleasing, codependency, and the inability to say no. Your true nature can often be replaced with a persona, an image you feel you have to reflect to the world. You are aware that you have extraordinary gifts. Combined with this and your genuine desire to do good, however, sometimes uncontrollable feelings of shame, guilt, and suppression are often present. You often ask yourself questions like:

Why should I be allowed to shine my light when others around me are suffering? I

Isn't it selfish to be empowered, self-loving, and self-respecting?

Shouldn't I put everyone's needs above my own, and be totally selfless?

The empath persona is about appearing selfless, caring, nurturing, intuitive, helpful, and devoted to others. The image all empaths want to project to the world is rooted in your innate qualities. So, in dreams, the persona will appear to you, to help you. It may appear as a specific dream character, a real-life waking character, a symbol, an image, or yourself. Many empaths struggle with stepping into their true persona due to the judgments of the outside world. It can be very hard to stay centered, aligned, and fully connected to your truth (when your nature is to naturally appease and sacrifice). In this respect, you can work with the persona archetype for healing on multiple levels. The ultimate goal of the empath is to heal and help, moreover to bring others up, inspire, and educate. Once you fully realize this truth, further truly coming to terms with the reality that *we are all one*, you will realize it is detrimental and harmful to not stand in your light. Shining your gifts is essential for self and others. Symbols, messages, and imagery are shown to us through dreams, specifically to how our empathy is being used, if it's currently blocked, and how to amplify and access it. Emotional blocks and wounds past, present, and future can be shown to us.

A key dream example indicating your persona would be this: Dreaming of being in a crowded place, holding on to your favorite toy as a child. You're feeling lost, confused, and alone... This dream message would be suggesting that, 1. you still have yet to become grounded, centered, and strong within, developing masculine strength and mental and intellectual power (to feel safe in a social situation). 2. you are too empathic, so your strong empathic personality is disconnecting you from those around you (the childhood toy represents a feeling of home, emotional connection, and comfort). Or. 3. You've yet to work on your boundaries or social anxiety, thus don't know how to show your true face to the world. Feeling lost, confused, and alone suggests the dream is showing you negative aspects of yourself, parts of you that need healing, releasing, or bringing to light. Your persona is your social identity or lack of it.

The Shadow

The shadow can be collective, individual, or unique to the empath personality. Your shadow self is everything hidden, repressed, and rejected, everything you want to deny and dismiss. It's the parts of your character, personality, and psyche, you perceive as ugly, the darker parts. They can represent fear, weakness, or insecurity, or qualities society deems weak or "lesser." In dreams, they can manifest as desires and memories that one simply does not wish to accept or integrate. Animal instincts and sexuality are integral parts of the collective shadow combined with the shadow aspect of an empath. The shadow may represent itself as a "lowly creature," like a dwarf or an animal representing primal instincts. Tigers, crocodiles, wasps, horses, and lions are often characterized here due to their connection to survival, primal instincts, and sexuality. The shadow amplifies and perpetuates when it is left unchecked, unhealed, and imbalanced. It can actually be dangerous when continuously denied or rejected. The more you resist, persists. We all have light and dark, good and evil, and opposing forces within us. Harmony, balance, and unity are required, and your shadow self is your ultimate route to wholeness.

The general rule is that the stronger we identify with our persona, the more we deny our shadow. Remember, your persona is how you wish to be seen by others, your positive light expression. The shadow is your negative or darker characteristics, likes, and desires. For empaths, all of the shadow traits explored in chapter 1 can be shown in dreams. They can appear as unique dream symbolism, scenes, and imagery, conversations, or through wisdom imparted by dream characters. Your Higher Self, soul, and psyche speak to you in dreams. In waking life, you pour copious amounts of time, love, and energy into a goal, cause, or project that enriches another's life. You're genuine in your desires to be of service, however you go too far. You forget yourself, becoming overly submissive or self-sacrificing. You forget your boundaries, people-please, and neglect personal joys, passions, and pleasures.

Recurring themes that are often present in an empath's life:-

- A suppression of sex, love, and desire
- A suppression of intimacy, self-love, and companionship
- A suppression of money, abundance, and financial prosperity
- A suppression of physical health, fitness, and vitality
- A suppression of material bliss, new opportunities, and living your dreams (from self-sacrifice)

The Anima and Animus

These are female and male aspects of yourself, respectively. Everyone possesses both feminine and masculine attributes, the anima and animus are not limited to being a Projection thus transforms into reflection, and woman or man. You're deeply aware by now that empaths have many talents rooted in feminine energy. You can therefore work with your anima to enhance and make sense of female qualities. You can work with animus to integrate and balance the (male) missing parts of you. When the anima or animus is unconscious and not seen, understood or accepted, we tend to *project* it outward onto others. One of the main ways this manifests is in relationships, specifically romantic and sexual relationships. Once you begin to have a synergistic relationship with your own inner-empath nature, only then can you *reflect* it out to the world, harmoniously and healthily.You mirror beautiful innate qualities- projection thus transforms into reflection. These two archetypes are intrinsic to empath healing and have been covered, organically, throughout this book.

The Divine Child

The divine child is your truest self in its purest form. It represents innocence, your sense of vulnerability, helplessness, hopefulness, and purity. It's your inner child coupled with your divine nature. It also symbolizes your goals, dreams, and aspirations, as well as your highest potential. In dreams, it can be represented by a child, baby, or infant or a group of any of these. This universal archetype is a fundamental part to the empath's journey; innocence, vulnerability and helplessness, goals and dreams, aspirations- reaching your highest potential with your inner child intact... this is ultimately the journey of an empath. In childhood, naivety, innocence, and a deep sense of majesty and wonder fill your life. You tend to wander around as some playful and free-spirited light giving super-human, always emparting deep wisdom and joy on others. Empaths are the type of people who will have a fleeting intuitive thought, a powerful instinctual feeling inside, and walk up to a stranger. There's a demeanor of magic and mystery surrounding you... Your intuition is strong , even when you don't understand it. And this means you act on intuitive hunches and gut feelings, which, as it should, keeps your inner child alive. The downside of being so innocent and carefree, embodying the energy of the Fool (Tarot) for many chapters of your life, is that you unconsciously take on a lot of stuff that doesn't belong to you through merging with others' auras and energy fields; their stories, pains, memories, traumas, joys, highs, lows... virtually everything and anything. You also attract narcissists and energy vampires (takers) and holistically have no sense of self, boundaries, or protective measures in place. (Although you are always spiritually protected!)

Your innocence allows you to see everyone as a reflection of you, a perfect mirror, but this can manifest as both negative (weak to no boundaries) and positive (you embody unconditional love) experiences. The divine child archetype may appear to:

1. Show you where you've been giving your power away, how and why you may still be acting childlike, naive, or immature, and what toxic or unhealthy cycles you've been repeating due to such innocence. Dreams show you the bad parts of yourself, moreover what you still need to heal.
2. Show you how you embody such universal and unconditional love, compassion, and sensitivity. Your kindness, generosity, and selflessness are reflected through the divine child.

As this archetype appears as a baby, infant, or child, the characteristics of the dream character will show you what messages are in store. Many insights and guidance can be shown to you, for example, a happy and joyous baby or child will suggest that you're in divine flow, you're living your best life in harmony with your purpose or true path. A crying baby or child suggests you are in a state of emotional imbalance, disharmony, or neglect of personal needs and self-care, or similar. A baby generally represents the younger version of you, so you can look back to your earliest waking life experiences. A child symbolizes your inner child. Symbolic of both helplessness and hopefulness, the divine child is here to remind you that you are always supported and protected. Your hopes, dreams, ambitions, aspirations, and long-term goals matter. Assuming that you are destined to follow "the path of the empath," these manifestations will present themselves as hopes, goals, and aspirations that lie in the realms of spirit, creativity, charity, service, animal welfare, environmentalism, healing, helping, or caring of some kind.

The Wise Old Man

This archetype is pretty self-explanatory; in dreams, he is represented by a masculine figure, like a father, teacher, or a masculine authority-type figure. The purpose of the wise old man is to offer insight, direction, and guidance rooted in traditions, self-authority, and masculine energy. It's in dreams where potent symbolism, guidance, and subconscious insights are available. The wise old man appears when you need wisdom or lessons in self-authority, self-leadership, assertiveness, direct communication, courage, confidence, self-esteem, and any masculine or expressive quality. The wise old man can appear as a seer, wizard, lecturer, elderly gentleman, teacher, judge, counselor, diplomat, or man of any type. Take note of all the imagery presented, the way he's dressed, how he speaks, what he says, his body language and aura, the feeling or mood you get from him, and so forth. This provides clues to the dream message.

The Great Mother

The wise old man's female counterpart, the great mother is the feminine aspect of your subconscious. She is the great nurturer and manifests in dreams as a grandmother, mother, fairy godmother, angel, light/positive female pixie, or any powerful and nurturing female figure. She is a strong spirit bringing empathy, caring, nurturance, compassion, gentleness, understanding, tolerance, and grace. Again, take note of her characteristics as outlined in the wise old man.

One other key way this universal archetype presents itself is as the dark witch. This can provide deep insights into negative expressions of your empath nature. Now, I am not talking about good witches, those real medicine women or magical healing fairy types. This is referring to the "evil" type- the green goblin, dark hat, black cloaked, and stereotypical bad witch. She has an evil face and a sinister expression, and is further clearly an omen of black magic or dark spellwork. This type of witch brings terror and fear and represents dominance, death, and seduction. This is the divine feminine 'gone wrong,' the manifestation of female attributes synergetic to the empath nature used with malicious intent, or out-of-control and unconscious. This is quite rare, as most empaths manage to make it out of their super-spacey, shadowy, and wounded space. But, some empaths move into adulthood 30- 40+, without healing their wounds or clearing past karmas and traumas. They thus circulate negative energy, the karmic actions of others (through a lack of deep healing and soul clearing), and cause chaos in the world around them. It's not conscious, an empath's intentions will *never* be to harm or hurt, so there's no karmic repercussions associated here. But the dark witch is a manifestation of the divine feminine, and this can create a lot of unnecessary suffering, in addition to time wasted.

Shadow themes related to the dark witch are seduction, unconscious feminine power, uncontrolled or unconscious sexuality, death, destruction, and raw emotions and desire. Lust comes into the dark witch, a character trait that occurs when you've denied or neglected your romantic or sexual needs for too long. Suppressed energy accumulates and can come out in an explosive nature, such as entering into a violent or abusive relationship (built off of false hopes and intentions), succumbing to fairytale love fantasies rooted in illusions and misdirection, or toxic cycles and behaviors linked to sexual needs, wants, and fantasies. If you were to ever have nightmares, as an empath, it is very likely that the bad dream is connected to this archetype. This is a unique frequency, however, and not all empaths will experience the dark witch in dreams. You can explore it consciously though. *Handy tip*: research the witch trials, medicine men and women/shamanic traditions, and divination, mysticism, and alchemy. Positive witches- light beings, work with herbs, plants, the natural world, in addition to natural universal healing energies. All witchcraft is rooted in the *light*, in a desire to heal or do good in the world. (This links with some of the empath blueprints, like the Seer, Spiritual Teacher, Telepath, Healer, and so on...)

The Trickster

As the name suggests, the trickster is the practical joker of the collective conscious energy field. The trickster shows itself as a pixie, evil elf, or dark spirit, not dangerous dark, but mischievous and playful. The trickster causes havoc, creating chaos and upheaval. He likes to play games. He may present himself in dreams if you have taken yourself too seriously, misjudged or over-reacted to a situation or person. As an empath, this applies to you more than others. Empaths are very serious, mellow, and emotionally intelligent, which means you like to hold space for others more than not. As a result, you can miss out on playfulness, colorful and upbeat energy, and inner fire and cerebral or intellectual energy. This creates blocks to love, abundance, and longevity. Wit, humor, and laughter or pure fun can be missed out on, especially and specifically when you're trying to embody such an advanced emotional frequency for self and others, as this is where you believe your healing powers lie. The trickster, therefore, comes to you when you need to lighten up, laugh more, and be more fun-loving and playful. Your dreams are here to help, guide, and remind you of the steps needed for wholeness and harmony in waking life. When you've been stuck in "too much depth and heart-to-heart bonding" mode for too long, the trickster arrives to remind you to be more fun. What's wrong with some good old-fashioned banter or giggles? Nothing.

Referring back to astrology, Libra is the most balanced sign, the sign of balance. Libra is not traditionally associated with the empath nature, but they are very empathic, compassionate, and sensitive to the needs of others. With the glyph of the Scales, Libra is a balanced, harmonious, and both left brain and right brain individual. They're skilled in cognitive abilities, problem-solving, intellect, logic, higher analytical and mental reasoning, wit, intellect, and all aspects of communication, as well as sensitivity, empathy, romance, kindness, and compassion. They're intuitive and imaginative. Ruled by Venus, the planet of love, beauty, female sexuality, pleasure, and romance, Libras are lovers. Venus is exalted in Pisces, the sign of the empath, and exalted means 'in its best position.' So, Libras are both superficial and deep, intellectual and romantic, and logical and intuitive. Their shadow side can be superficiality coupled with egotistical and narcissistic energy, qualities the empath blueprint lacks. Why shar ethos? Because, as the colorful and empathic but equally cerebral and intellectual sign of *balance*, who is known for being incredibly positive, upbeat, and colorful, you can learn a lot from this sign. Superficiality is a trait that can help you in a lot of social situations, as well as to overcome social anxiety, fear of large crowds or public spaces, and any type of insecurities or hyper-emotionalism.

There's nothing wrong with being superficial every once in a while, dear empath. Superficiality can move blocked or stagnant energy up from your Sacral (emotional center), help you to see new and fresh perspectives, and introduce more light, color, and fun into your life. The trickster archetype, therefore, can be learned about, integrated, and meditated on to enhance the missing qualities in your life. His energy is not specifically masculine- laughter, wit, and humor can be very feminine, too. However, relating to the empath nature we can suggest that this archetype is effective for increasing masculine energy, as well all aspects relating to *light*-heartedness. Remember that lightness is symbolic of yang or masculine energy.

The Ego and The Self

The ego is one of the main archetypes of the personality and is known as the center of consciousness. It is the 'I,' the aspect of self that is central in daily life. It is the part that relates to the psyche combined with all things personal; personal experiences, lessons, and core life teachings throughout the entire human journey. The other part of the psyche is the unconscious. Short and sweet, empaths don't have big egos. On the contrary, you seem to lack ego, being too selfless, too self-sacrificing, too giving, too submissive, and so on. If you have any lessons to learn regarding your ego, your subconscious will certainly show you in your dreams.

The self is arguably the most important archetype as it represents the *whole personality*. It is the union of the conscious and unconscious mind. It is centeredness, balanced energy, harmony, and the merging and unification of opposites. Duality becomes oneness with a healed and integrated self. In dreams, the self is depicted as a circle, mandala, crystal, or stone (impersonal), or as a royal couple, divine child, or some other symbol of divinity, such as Christ, Buddha, or other great spiritual teachers (personal). These symbols of the self are all representations of wholeness, completion, unification, and reconciliation of opposites. They are therefore great for the empath psyche. Becoming in tune with your whole self is therefore best for your *ultimate and unified expression….* without repressions or suppressions. The self whole and integrated is you *self-mastered*. The Self leads you back to your highest potential. Referring back to the dream symbolism of the self, you can work with this imagery in waking life too. Let's briefly delve into these.

Circle: A circle symbolizes pure consciousness, the infinite and eternal nature of life and self. The starting and ending points circle round on each other, leading to wholeness, unification, and integration.

Mandala: A mandala is a beautiful art piece created in meditation, with mindful intent. It has healing benefits, being observed or tuned into for self-development, healing, and self-care purposes. Mandalas are spiritual, sacred, and ritual representations of the microcosm and macrocosm often used in Buddhism and Hinduism.

Crystals and gemstones: Crystals and gemstones have many healing benefits, two in particular that best represent the self being Clear Quartz and the Diamond. Clear Quartz connects to the Crown chakra and is symbolic of the kundalini, wholeness, and integration. The Diamond is the hardest and strongest, moreover one of the most rare gemstones on earth. It signifies divinity, self-realization, and universal love on the highest planes.

Royal Couple: A royal couple shows one of two things. Firstly, it represents that you're ready for a relationship, for a divine union, and a real sacred soulmate bond. It's the joining of two healed, beautiful, and self-sovereign souls. Secondly, it signifies the unification of polar opposite forces within, yin and yang, the divine feminine and masculine.

Divine Child: A divine child signifies divine strength, power, and self-alignment. It's both your inner child healed and healthy- happy, joyous, and content, and the possible birth of an extraordinary creation. This could be an actual child or children, motherhood, or fertility, or a creative project, collaborative venture, or partnership.

Christ, Buddha, and Spiritual Teachers: Spiritual teachers and religious deities are final symbols of the self, and represent your belief systems in their integrated and completed state. They impart a lot of wisdom and profound insights on you. Alternatively, they appear when you need direction and guidance, when there's a loss of self or you're going through challenging times.

Best Careers for Empaths

Now that you've completed the "empath journey," returning back to your center, wholeness, and inner harmony and equilibrium, you can start to examine some of the best jobs, careers, and vocations. These are intrinsically tied into the empath blueprints on pages 12- 24. The world needs more of your purity, natural beauty, and unique way of perceiving and experiencing the world. Your compassion, kindness, soul, sincerity, and depth of spirit are unmatched, and this can help you thrive in a number of situations and professions. Hopefully by now you've learned that narcissists, energy vampires, and other toxic personalities have no role in your life. You do not need to be anyone's emotional dumping ground, put up with anyone's BS, and that you have immense power to respect and protect yourself. Below are some of the best careers for an empath. Do make sure you've worked on your shadow self first, however! This is an essential step to self-mastery, so you can be of the greatest service in the world.

- Musician
- Artist
- Writer
- Photographer
- Creative Filmmaker or Director
- Graphic Designer
- Psychologist

- Philosopher
- Nurse
- Physician
- Veterinarian
- Holistic or Complementary Therapist
- Massage Therapist
- Dream Therapist
- Social or Support Worker
- Animal Welfare or Rescue
- Charity Worker or Leader
- Non-Profit Organization Leader or Worker
- Environmentalist
- Gardener
- Campaigner
- Speaker
- Teacher
- Life Coach
- Counselor
- Healer
- Hospice Worker
- Spiritual Teacher, Speaker, or Healer
- Tarot Reader
- Psychic
- Shaman, Seer, or Mystical Healer

Conclusion

The world can often be a cold and harsh place, there is so much injustice, barbarity, and evil. People act from ego, live in a state of separation, and succumb to illusory fears and projections. We're supposed to be mirrors of one another, reflecting positive qualities, and healing one another. Yet this isn't the case. Fortunately, this is where empaths step in! Empaths are powerful creatures with amazing healing, counseling, and caregiving gifts, least to mention extraordinary levels of creativity and imagination. No matter your soul mission, life path, or destiny, you are intended to choose a vocation or mode of service that allows your unique *empathy* to shine. It's your job and responsibility to ride the waves, become self-mastered, and work through your shadow, so you can step into greatness. Empathy is the gift of feeling things deeply, connecting to others psychically and telepathically, and merging with others in a way that inspires growth and healing. You are wise beyond your years...

In the words of Albert Einstein, a Pisces I synchronously share the same birthdate with, *"Everybody is a genius. But if you judge a fish by its ability to climb a tree, it will live its whole life believing that it's stupid."*

✦

AFTERWORD

Enjoyed this book? I hope so. As an empath, I feel it's essential to no longer live in ignorance or denial. Empath healing is core to your journey and self-evolution into stardom and greatness. I have a lot of free videos, both face-to-camera and audio only, available on my Youtube channel, *The Dream & Spirit Weaver*. You might want to visit the 'most popular' to see what can spark your Crown…

My other books:

A Message from Source: 33 poems exploring consciousness, our connection to one another, and the universe as a whole. *My debut book won the Local Legend National Writing Competition in 2014.*

A Story of One: A sequel to *A Message from Source*, which delves into tantra, mysticism, healing, higher consciousness, love, intimacy, friendship, community, and soulmate bonds.

Spirit Animals of the Star Signs: Power Animals of the Zodiac: With 52 reviews at the time of writing this book, this game changing "one-of-a-kind" book on spirit animals and astrology was written during my travels through South America in 2022. I began writing in the sacred Mayan lands of Mexico, continued in the mountainous rainforests of Monteverde Costa Rica, and finished in the Amazon Jungle in Ecuador. This book is so in depth it's been described as the holy grail of guides!

Pisces Dream Astrology: The Dreamer (Old Souls Dreams): A book exclusively on Pisces, the 12th and final sign, the mystic, healer, and dreamer… (I myself am a Pisces Sun with my Venus in Pisces too.) *This book can also be consulted for dream symbolism and exploration.*

Mental Health Issues of the Star Signs & Zodiac: Let's Get Triggered, Heal, and Evolve… Together: *Not for the faint-hearted*; this book is a one-of-a-kind deep-sea dive into the mental health patterns and blueprints of each star sign.

52 Tantric Tips for Ultimate Intimacy from an Energy Master: Exploring Tantric Intimacy; Merging the Lower Primal Self and Higher Spiritual Self for Your Best Sex Life!- As the title signifies…

If you have the paperback copy, all of these books can be found on Amazon! <3

Printed in Great Britain
by Amazon